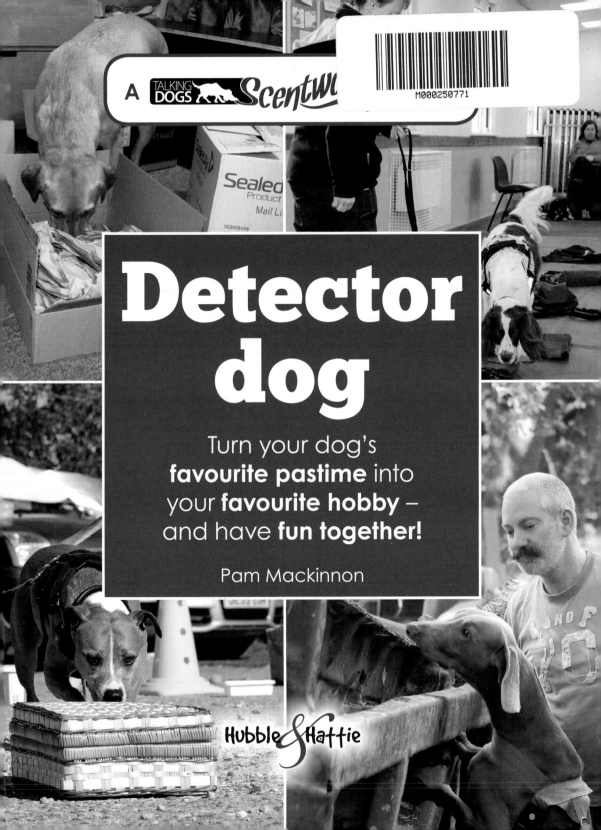

A Scentw...

M000250771

Detector dog

Turn your dog's **favourite pastime** into your **favourite hobby** – and have **fun together!**

Pam Mackinnon

Hubble & Hattie

The Hubble & Hattie imprint was launched in 2009 and is named in memory of two very special Westie sisters owned by Veloce's proprietors. Since the first book, many more have been added to the list, all with the same underlying objective: to be of real benefit to the species they cover, at the same time promoting compassion, understanding and respect between all animals (including human ones!) All Hubble & Hattie publications offer ethical, high quality content and presentation, plus great value for money.

More great books from Hubble & Hattie –

www.hubbleandhattie.com

First published April 2017 by Veloce Publishing Limited, Veloce House, Parkway Farm Business Park, Middle Farm Way, Poundbury, Dorchester, Dorset, DT1 3AR, England. Fax 01305 250479/email info@hubbleandhattie.com/web www.hubbleandhattie.com ISBN: 978-1-845849-63-4 UPC: 6-36847-04963-8 ©Pam Mackinnon & Veloce Publishing Ltd 2017.
Readers with ideas for books about animals, or animal-related topics, are invited to write to the editorial director of Veloce Publishing at the above address. British Library Cataloguing in Publication Data - A catalogue record for this book is available from the British Library. Typesetting, design and page make-up all by Veloce Publishing Ltd on Apple Mac. Printed in India by Replika Press.

Contents

Acknowledgements and Dedication

Acknowledgements

My thanks to all of the dogs and handlers who I've had the pleasure of working with over the last six years. Working with the huge variety of breeds, temperaments and ages of dog have stretched and strengthened my knowledge more than you know. Working with people of different ages and abilities has helped me hone my training to make them accessible to everyone, so that nobody is excluded from our game.

Thanks to Sue Sternberg for kick-starting my brain and asking the question: "Why don't you teach scentwork?"

Thanks to my Talking Dogs Scentwork® Accredited Trainers who help me share the scentwork love.

Thanks to the photographers who allowed me to include their images: Bob Atkins, Wayne Holt, and *Your Dog* Magazine, and to Ellis Donovan for his illustrations.

Dedication

To my ever-patient, ever-joyous, ever-loyal companions, Cherry Blossom and Ella. Bouncy, smiley, snuggly and sniffy: you keep me playful.

And to Air Dog Ash. My friend, my colleague and my teacher throughout our detection adventures and beyond.

Pam and Air Dog Ash.

What is Talking Dogs Scentwork®?

TALKING DOGS Scentwork® (TDS) is about teaching your dog to find a specific scent. It is a free-flowing search style that allows a dog to cover complex areas efficiently and effectively. The handler works to support the dog and ensure the whole area has been cleared: ie there are no hidden articles remaining.

Talking Dogs Scentwork® would never have come into being were it not for a road trip conversation with my great friend, Sue Sternberg. Her suggestion that I offer some scentwork training was the first time I'd ever considered using the skills I'd learned as a drug detector handler for HM Customs & Excise (as it was called) with my pet dog clients and colleagues. On reflection, however, I realised that I'd always used it in informal ways: playing scentwork games to help dogs cope with stressful, exciting or distracting situations.

I began by introducing occasional small searches as a part of my adult dog training classes. Much to my surprise and delight, people really loved it! The dogs were animated and excited about working, and their owners were amazed at the scentwork skill their dogs displayed. I quickly realised that in order to allow everyone to participate, I would have to adapt some of the techniques to suit those dogs who had not been specially selected for their high drive, confidence, and willingness to work. By incorporating parts of other dog training disciplines, such as gundog work, and being flexible with what they had to find (using food as well as toys), I developed Talking Dogs Scentwork®.

Within the dog world there are a variety of search styles, each adapted to a specific task. Search and Rescue (SAR) primarily uses air scenting in order to cover large areas. It would be ridiculous to ask a dog to sniff every blade of grass in order to find someone lost on a mountain, for example, so, instead, he must cast around to quickly find a scent he can latch on to; then off he goes with the handler following.

Working Trials search squares ask the dog to search alone for random articles that have human scent - sometimes their handler's;

sometimes not – rather than using one specific, taught scent. The articles that the dog is asked to find and retrieve are often incongruous to the area: he might be asked to find a wooden or metal article in a grassy area, for example. The retrieve is crucial in order for the team to qualify (gain enough points to progress through the competition).

Obedience scent discrimination always asks the dog to identify one specific human scent on a cloth from a pattern of unscented cloths laid out on the ground. The dog doesn't have to search the area to find the cloth; he has to work over the cloths that are clearly presented without any help from his handler, who stands back and cannot support him during the search.

Tracking, for fun or competition, requires the dog to identify disturbance in the environment, such as trampled grass, and lead the handler along that trail of disturbance searching for articles placed along or at the end of the trail. Unlike working dogs, these dogs will be brought to the start of the track. Once they hit the trail, they follow it until they find the person or articles. The handler follows the dog by holding a long tracking line attached to the dog's harness, so will be far back, relying on the dog to find the right clues and lead them to the article(s). These dogs will use a combination of air and ground scenting.

Operational detector dogs, such as those in Customs or military forces, are required to find a variety of known scents in a variety of areas, indoors and out, at various heights and in various conditions, working as a team with their handler.

Each working style will suit particular dogs, and will be selected on the basis of the work required. Talking Dogs Scentwork® uses all of these methods, allowing the dog to learn new strategies, build on favoured ones, and work together with his handler to reach a common goal, which is why the system is suitable for all dogs. The teamwork is what helps make this such a fun activity for both dog and handler.

Who can do it?

Everyone can participate in this style of scentwork, as the searches can be adapted to the skills, experience, and ability of both handler and dog. Some people love to watch their dogs searching without any help from them: they hide something, then send their dog into the area to find it. Others want to be part of the search, supporting their dog to find ever more challenging 'hides.' By tailoring each search to the participants, everyone wins. So, people or dogs with mobility issues can join in, dogs who do not like to play with toys can search for specific food 'finds' instead, and folks with ambitions to work professionally can hone their skills.

During my time as a professional drug detector dog handler I worked English Springer Spaniels: speedy, brave and hard-working dogs who wanted to search all day long. Many companion dogs do not have this intense, almost obsessive, motivation to work, and so, from an operational perspective, would not be accepted as a detector dog. And from the point of view of a dog as a companion animal, the intense drive to be constantly busy can be undesirable and difficult to live with.

Through working with companion dogs and their owners, my understanding of scentwork increased tenfold, as observing and supporting dogs not specifically chosen for scentwork has allowed me to gain a much deeper understanding of how they work, and what they need to be successful in this area.

Scentwork is not limited to specific breeds, ages, physical abilities or courage: some of the loveliest searches I've witnessed have been by a Great Dane, a Jack Russell Terrier, and a Whippet. Scentwork helps owners learn to be sensitive to their dog's body language and state of mind. Subtle changes in tail position or speed of movement can be the first signs that a dog has found the scent. Through careful observation of their dogs, owners learn to spot these signals and, in turn, identify what their dogs are saying and feeling in day-to-day situations; not just when searching.

Confidence plays a huge part in scentwork. By recognizing differences in their dog's confidence level, owners can better help them reach emotional equilibrium. For owners with physical restrictions, scentwork is a wonderful way to enjoy encouraging their dog to be active, without necessarily being too active themselves. Working with handlers in wheelchairs or with walking aids helped me reassess the priorities of the search system, and modify and adjust the search area, cues and supports as necessary.

Dogs with physical limitations can also successfully participate in Talking Dogs Scentwork®. I have worked with dogs who are deaf, blind, and even deaf-blind; amputees, and dogs with chronic joint or back problems. We adapt the searches and the handling to accommodate issues like these, and to maximize the dog's abilities.

And dogs with mental or emotional issues can participate, too. Dogs who do not relish the company of other dogs can search to their heart's content without the worry of having to interact with another dog. Dogs who are nervous, and whose anxiety has inhibited learning, have successfully learned my system, and been able to work in places where previously they could not. This activity builds confidence and can help dogs improve their emotional state, both during and after scentworking.

So, who can do Talking Dogs Scentwork®? Everyone. And everyone can benefit from it.

Benefits of Talking Dogs Scentwork®

Talking Dogs Scentwork® is mentally exhausting, and can tire out your dog very quickly. Scentwork requires great concentration, which is why dogs get tired so quickly. With physical exercise, the more he does it the fitter your dog becomes; he doesn't become more tired. Combining physical health with mental effort will, however, result in a tired dog. I often see clients who complain that their dog never settles, even after a long walk. But 20 minutes of scentwork and their dog will be snoring on the sofa, satisfied and happy.

Imagine a really rainy day. You've been out with your dog once, and you've both finally dried off. The question 'Do we really have to go out there again?' is one you don't want to answer, and if you do some scentwork instead you won't have to. I rarely advocate scentwork instead of all physical exercise, but, for some dogs, staying at home is their only or best option, and working on their mental well-being is just as important as physical exercise ... and is much more often neglected.

How often do you walk your dog? Every day? Great. How often do you train him? A couple of times a week? What does he do with his brain the rest of the time? Sadly, boredom is a fact of life for the majority of companion dogs. Banish boredom with Talking Dogs Scentwork®.

This activity is also an excellent way to reconnect with your dog, especially if your relationship has gone through rocky times. It builds trust, and can help speed up bonding with newly-rescued dogs. And it helps build concentration in young or impulsive dogs. The beauty of scentwork is that each dog works to his or her own ability, as handlers, trainers and assistants constantly respond and fine-tune the search according to what the individual dog needs.

And, of course, it's FUN! Dogs are allowed to be dogs and engage in an activity that owners can often find annoying or worrying. For example, it may appear that a dog who

is walking with his head down, sniffing the ground is not paying attention to his walker; likewise if he should pull on the lead in an effort to reach an interesting scent. There is also sometimes the concern that, should a dog find the scent of another animal when off-lead, he will immediately tear off after the rabbit or deer he scents. Instead of battling against their dog's natural desire to search, owners can subtly harness and control how it's done.

Search techniques can help greatly with daily training and many behavioural issues. From improving recalls to learning to cope with traffic, scentwork is an adaptable, effective activity to add to your toolbox, and your dog's skill set.

NB: For ease of reading, the text refers to a dog as a male throughout: however, female is implied at all times.

Visit Hubble and Hattie on the web: www.hubbleandhattie.com
hubbleandhattie.blogspot.co.uk
• Details of all books • Special offers • Newsletter • New book news

How TDS works

How the dog's nose works - a quick guide

THE DOG inhales air, and the scent particles carried within it, through his anterior nares (nostrils), which dilate as he breathes in. The scented air passes through the dog's nose (a bony nasal cavity divided into two chambers by the septum), and is warmed and moistened through the turbinates (two spongy bones which are rolled into a cone shape and sit each side of the septum). The air hits a small patch of tissue in the back of the nasal cavity called the olfactory epithelium, which is thirty times bigger in dogs than in humans. The olfactory receptor (OR) cells, neurons (twice the number in dogs, compared to humans) in the olfactory epithelium act as sensory signalling cells due to the cilia (cellular antennae) on their surface, which are in direct contact with the air.

This causes a chemical stimulus that initiates an electrical signal, firing neurons along the olfactory nerve to the olfactory bulb. The olfactory bulb is the part of the central nervous system through which the signal is carried to the brain; specifically to the limbic system where interpretation of the scent begins. It has been estimated that as much as a third of the dog's brain is dedicated to scenting.

How scent works

The dog's sense of smell is truly astounding. We still don't know for sure by how much exactly, but it is thought to be between 10,000 and 100,000 times greater than ours. The olfactory cortex in dogs - which determines what the scent is and its relevance - is thought to be forty times greater than that in us. Everything has a scent, and how that scent moves around an area is often not obvious to us non-canines.

The three main elements of how scent works are -

- The scent picture
- The search article
- The scent itself

- and looking at these in detail will help clarify what your dog is working with.

Air scenting.

• The scent picture

First of all, the movement of scent – or 'plume' – is known as the scent picture, which can only be detected by the dog and not by the handler. Whilst it is thought that scent can exist in a vacuum, movement – usually caused by air – is required to create a scent picture or trail: where there is air and airflow, there will be scent.

For example, wind or breeze will carry scent, as will the air all around us. Have you ever been driving and suddenly smelt smoke? Is the car on fire? Is the engine going to blow? Once we've discounted these possibilities, we begin to look outside the car ... and then we see it, way in the distance: a small bonfire in someone's garden. Airflow is what allows the

scent to reach us over great distances, and as smoke is one of the scents that is historically very important to humans, we are excellent at detecting and reacting to it.

Air movement indoors is equally important, but more predictable. Each time a door opens and closes, a dog wags his tail, or a person moves through an area to hide an article for him to find, the air is disturbed and scent is circulated.

Temperature is extremely important in connection with scent. Hot environments distribute scent, making it large and fluid, whereas cold environments contain scents, making them small and more static.

Think of the gutsy smells that waft out of busy kitchens compared to the minimal odour of a cold store. The heat of a kitchen speeds up movement of the scent particles, causing the air to rise, and so draws out the scent and distributes it freely around a room. People moving around in the kitchen will also disturb the air, creating further distribution. This means that a dog is more likely to hit the scent early into the search, but might take longer to track it back to the source.

But in a cold store devoid of people, scent particles will move slowly. Cold air sinks so will take much longer to move away from the source, requiring a dog to carry out a more detailed search in order to pick up the initial scent, although, as it will be closer to the source, he should track it back faster. As a result, it could take the same amount of time to search and clear both areas, despite their very different conditions.

The scent picture will be affected if the search article is near a heater or a window; outdoors or indoors; if the weather is hot or cold; windy or still. The handler should be aware of temperature and movement of air, as the dog certainly will be! One of the best times to catch a glimpse into the invisible world of scent is when a dog is air scenting, as his nose

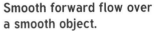

Smooth forward flow over a smooth object.

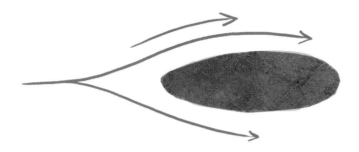

follows the scent trail as it moves through the air. Watch him as he tracks the scent of an animal in the woods ... or follows the smell of a roast as it comes out of the oven.

The Kinetic Theory of Gases tells us that particles move in a straight line until they collide with something. Depending on what this is, the scent will be distributed in a variety of ways, though will become weaker the further it travels from its source. As gases have many of the same properties as liquids, it may be easier to consider how water responds when it collides with solid objects.

When the sea moves over small objects such as rocks or pebbles, the water simply flows over and under them, and so will air. Smooth objects allow the air to travel neatly over them without much disturbance, but hard edges tend to create small splashes that rise up and away as the water or air moves over the top of the object.

Consider where the water goes when the sea meets cliffs. It can't go over the cliffs, so it comes into contact with them, rises up and out a little, and then drops. Water is heavier than air, of course, so drops faster, but air will behave the same way when it hits a wall, moving up, out, and down.

If the flow cannot move through, around or under an object, it will first travel upward before falling back down.

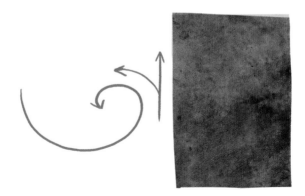

Sharp edges cause the flow to disperse up and out as it travels over the object.

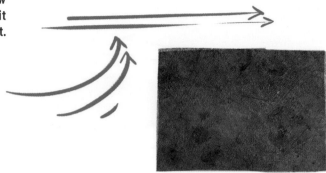

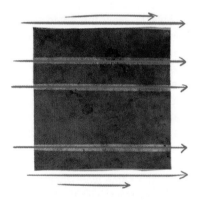

If the flow is strong, and the object short enough, it can travel up and over. It can also move under and through, seeking out gaps in the structure.

Next, consider what happens when the sea hits the promenade. It moves up the wall and maybe over the top, continuing on in its original path. Likewise, air hitting a low obstacle – a piece of furniture, say – will move up, over, and on. Of course, if there are cracks in the promenade, some of the water will also continue straight on, moving into the cracks, just as air will if there is any space for it to move under or through the obstacle. This is not an either/or situation: air can move in many directions at once.

To figure out the likely direction of airflow, look for objects that will affect the air's passage – walls, trees, and furniture – and airflow sources: open doors and windows, vents, fans, and people moving around.

Just as water will soak into some materials but pass over others, so, too, does air. Cloth, wood and plaster will soak up scent as it is carried in the area, while brick, metal and concrete retain very little (this may change depending on the temperature of these materials). When working indoors, ceiling height will affect temperature and air movement, as will the ambient temperature of the room.

Imagine a scented article located in an open cardboard box in the middle of a room. Without any influence from airflow, the scent would disperse evenly in all directions, but there

Scent travels up the wall due to the heat of the radiator. (Courtesy Bob Atkins/Your Dog Magazine)

cause some of the scent to travel up towards the ceiling, while some of it might move *towards* the heat. An open window to the left of the article could be letting in cold air, which would cause the scent to drop, but would also provide an opening for it to move through, so some might rise up and outward, although more air would become cold so drop down. A wooden floor would absorb more scent than brick walls, and a high vaulted ceiling could hold the warm air as it rises and hits the cold air in the ceiling space.

Can you see how complicated this is? Happily, a dog can work out all of this very quickly, pinpointing the area with the strongest scent (which, in the foregoing scenario, I would suggest may be up and to the right of the article), then working it back to the source. And this is why we leave scenting to the dog, with the handler taking the supporting role.

When working outdoors, the main factor will be the weather. I've talked about the effect of heat and cold, but what about rain, wind, frost or snow?

Scent generally rises to the top of water. Static or stagnant water allows scent to rise, but rain is constantly moving, so quickly washes away scent. Scent can float on streams but, as the stream is flowing, it doesn't remain for long. Tidal 'hides' have proven interesting, with scent remaining at the underwater hide, despite forward movement of the tide. Frost and snow cool the air and cause the scent to move slowly, though does contain the scent, preventing it from dissipating too quickly and giving the dog a good chance of locating it if he gets close enough. Scent can also sit on top of snow, allowing the dog to locate it with ease. Scent underneath snow is much trickier to locate: it can be done, but only if the dog's

would be airflow as the handler and dog would be causing air to move, never mind any other influences (a wagging tail alone causes quite a bit of air turbulence!). For example, opening a door towards us and closing it behind us when entering a room could pull air out and then push it back in. A fan heater pumping out hot air to the right of the hidden article would push hot air towards the article, which would

nose and nasal passages aren't too cold and dry, which would prevent them working effectively. Ideally, dogs should have frequent access to water before, after, and sometimes during, a search in order to stay hydrated and keep the nose and nasal passages lubricated.

Wind is probably the most interesting and challenging weather condition to work with, as it takes scent to all sorts of unimaginable places; allows a dog to locate a scent and then carries it away again, and it moves fast, far and often unpredictably: very difficult. It is for this reason that I introduce scentwork indoors rather than outside, as novice dogs who locate a scent, and then have it suddenly disappear, can find this off-putting and unrewarding. We should always set up dogs for success, so start scentwork indoors.

So, dogs working in cold, stormy weather can have some of the toughest searches. Worth remembering when next you see an SAR team on the news ...

As a brief rule of thumb, these are the main points to consider –

- Temperature

- Scent will generally rise on hot days, indoors or outside especially when it hits a wall or solid vertical surface

- Indoors, scent will move around windows, doors and heaters, and fans and air conditioners if switched on

- Scent will soak into soft materials as it passes over or through them

- Scent will continue to move past shiny, hard materials as it passes over them

- Scent tends to pool in the corners of rooms as it has limited access to other areas (it keeps bouncing off the two walls that make up the corners, and/or the ceiling or floor)

- Damp, or wet areas can often retain strong scent for short periods

- When outdoors, work your dog into the wind to give him the best chance of picking up the scent

- Prevent people from walking around your search area as this will disturb the scent picture – unless you are doing it specifically to increase the challenge of the search

- Try to ensure that airflow in the room is as consistent as possible. If you move a box as you are concealing the scented article inside it, air disturbance around the box will be greater than around other boxes/things in the room. This may result in your dog being more attracted to the disturbance than the scent, looking for that in future searches, rather than the scent. To prevent this, move other boxes/things in the room also to create the same disturbance of air around them

All of the above must be considered when supporting a dog searching for the source of a scent. Remember: only the dog can see the scent picture, so follow his lead. Trust him!

- **The search article**
The search article has its own scent picture. Not unsurprisingly, porous, softer materials soak up and release scent more easily than impermeable, hard materials, so locating a metal object is likely to be more difficult than locating one made of towelling, say.

The amount of scent an article gives out increases according to its size: ie the bigger the article the greater the scent, and vice versa. Using soft, scented articles in the initial

The scentwork mouse. (Courtesy Wayne Holt)

dogs, fleece tug toys are an excellent vehicle for holding scent and providing a great game at the end of the search.

Try to use the squashiest, smallest toy you can, as very long, chunky or solid toys can be limiting when it comes to finding good hiding places for them. Ensure that they are not so small, though, that your dog could swallow them: safety is paramount. Toys covered in tennis ball felt are also good as this soaks up the scent nicely, though be aware that the rubber can be rather pungent, so quickly move on to other scented articles, not just tennis balls and the like.

stages of scentwork means more scent is released when the dog plays with them at the end of a search. Biting down on the article releases more scent, and the relevance of scent is reinforced by your dog's enjoyment of the game. You can use soft toys, such as the small mice we use in my workshops, which are about 6cm (2½ inches) long, or, for bigger

Whichever article you choose, remember that your dog is learning to search for the *scent* on the article, and not the actual article, which means that, as he becomes more experienced, you could use a mouse, a tuggy, and a tennis

Different materials retain different amounts of scent.

Bags of dried catnip.

scent itself, which, if we can smell, your dog certainly can, and if we cannot smell it, your dog probably can. I start dogs on dried catnip, a distinctive, strong-smelling herb that isn't available to most dogs on a daily basis: my preference is for Kong® Naturals Premium Catnip. It may sound obvious, but don't choose scents that dogs find unpleasant, as these will deter him from searching. Dogs often dislike citrus or bitter odours, and I have found that many dogs do not like the smell of aniseed, despite it being a popular scent in some nosework competitions. Due to the vomeronasal organ (Jacobson's organ), dogs can taste what they smell, so, when choosing a scent, allow your dog to sniff it first. If he recoils or backs away, don't use it, and if there is no reaction or mild interest, you can use it. A colleague chose ginger as her dog's scent: an excellent choice as she was able to start with a food reward (a form of ginger cake), and then change over to ginger-scented articles.

Scents used in nosework competitions (trials) are often oil based (a good carrier that easily releases scent), but essential oil or liquid-based scents present some practical problems, the first and most important of which is safety. A great many substances and oils are toxic to dogs, including anise, peppermint and thyme, especially when undiluted. Of course, a dog should never be allowed to ingest the scent or oils during scentwork, and any amounts accidentally ingested would be very small (some are even found in some dog foods and treats in very dilute forms). However, if you have taught your dog to search for an oil-based scent, what happens if he comes across the bottle of scent that you thought you'd safely stored out of his reach?

One of our handlers recently recounted the tale of the morning she went for a shower, only to find that, whilst showering, her clever Spaniel had climbed onto a chair, opened a cupboard, and chewed into the tub of catnip

ball, but with only one of them being scented. Or you could put out two unscented tennis balls and a new article that is scented. Furry pencil cases make great scent toys because, if you need to scent something quickly, you can pop some of the scent inside the pencil case and off you go. These little changes help ensure that your dog is really searching for the scent, rather than assuming that it will always be on the same article. The only constant is the taught scent, which is what your dog will search for.

As your dog becomes ever more experienced, change the scented article to something made from a harder substance, such as plastic, wood or rubber, before trying your dog on scented stone and metal. These materials soak up and release less scent, so make for more challenging searches. Eventually, your dog can look for the scent alone, by simply smearing it onto a surface in the search area. This provides the ultimate challenge – for both dog and handler.

• **The scent**

The final element of this aromatic trio is the

stored there. While there was some mess to clear up (and I doubt she could ever use the room for scentwork again), her dog was unharmed. A cautionary tale, though, for anyone thinking of teaching their dog to search for a toxic substance.

I always prefer to work on the side of caution, and recommend that you thoroughly research the substance you would like to use to ensure it is safe for your dog, and you are fully aware of how much care is required.

It is also important to point out that our dogs are searching for fun, so there is never any reason to ask them to search for anything that could be toxic, including substances such as gun oil, drugs or tobacco. Even some herbs are contra-indicated for some dogs. For example, rosemary has been connected with provoking adverse effects in dogs with epilepsy. *Do your homework; keep your dog safe.*

If you do decide to use an oil-based scent, be aware that it is very easy to use too much oil, and so make the scent extremely strong. This can flood a dog's scent receptors, and actually make it more difficult for him to locate the scent source, and will also cause greater distribution of the scent particles, contaminating anything it touches or gets close to.

For example, if you hide a very heavily-scented, oil-based article in your living room behind the sofa, it will contaminate the whole sofa - and perhaps even the entire room – very quickly, thus making it very challenging to conduct future searches in that area. Liquid-based scents, such as oil or liquid catnip, soak into everything close by, via smell and physical contact. However a dry, non-oil-based scent, such as dried catnip, will not cause the same level of contamination.

Another practical issue is that of storage. Scented search articles should be kept individually in an airtight container, preferably made of tin or glass, as neither of these will let scent seep out. Plastic containers *can* be used, but the longer they are used the more contaminated they will become, and eventually the scent will leach through and out of them, contaminating the surrounding area. Tin is the best material as it is light and portable, although liquid will corrode it before too long, resulting in rust which has a scent. Your dog may therefore start to search for traces of rust as well as the scent you intended. Other scents that come into contact with the scented article will contaminate it, so by minimizing crossover in both directions (from and to the scented article), the risk of contamination and confusion is minimized. In my experience, dried catnip stored in a metal container is the ideal combination.

If you want to teach your dog to find more than one scent, your chances of success increase if you use separate articles for each scent, and don't wash a toy previously scented with catnip, then give it a different scent. Using separate articles will ensure that your dog detects each scent, rather than honing in on the strongest one, and does not learn that all scents you want him to find have a common component: ie he can always detect the same strong scent, no matter which one you actually think he is searching for. If this does happen, when you use a new toy that contains only the new scent, your dog may not indicate he has found the source as he cannot detect the original, strong scent he knows and recognises.

However, I do not recommend teaching a dog to find multiple scents. Doing so doesn't necessarily increase the fun of scenting, and brings with it many practical problems, usually concerned with avoiding cross-contamination. Instead of using multiple scents, searches can be made more challenging by reducing the strength of the scent or the size of the scent picture; extending the length of searches, and

Talking Dogs Scentwork® starter kit.

varying height and location of 'hides.' More on this later.

Ensure that the toys and scents you use are safe for your dog, as he will probably come into contact with both, especially when you conduct proactive free searches with active indications (see Glossary for explanation of terms).

Adapt favourite scentwork soft toys with Velcro® or press stud fastenings to make it easy to insert scent inside them, should you want to use a toy quickly; ie you don't have a toy 'cooking' in the scent tin. Some cat toys have Velcro® sealed pockets that are ideal for this purpose. Avoid toys that already contain catnip as this can't be removed to wash the toy, so are only good for one or two searches.

Some people like to use their own scent on the article (this is used in obedience competitions on scent cloths). However, I do not recommend using the handler's scent for Talking Dogs Scentwork®. Everything in your house and car – your belongings, your dog's belongings, toys, etc – will carry your scent: a contamination that will be at a low level for some things (such as wooden furniture and unread books sitting on the shelf), but at a high level in your bedding or favourite chair.

Working your dog in a contaminated area such as your home makes it much more difficult for him to find the article he's looking for, as not only will he have to identify the scent, he'll also have to discriminate between scents.

For example, he has to figure out that your favourite chair is not the article, but that the human-scented mouse behind the chair is.

Interestingly, when you go to search areas not already contaminated by your scent, the opposite occurs: your scent is not strong enough for the novice dog to detect. Unless the dog is searching a finite number of scent cloths, one of which he knows will definitely hold your scent, this scent is too weak, too difficult for him to find. Of course, once he becomes an experienced scentworker, he will be able to detect it easily, but at the initial stages of scentwork he needs a stronger scent to help build his skills and confidence.

When I worked Customs dogs they were trained to find four scents: cannabis, amphetamines, cocaine, and heroin. Training always began with cannabis as this has the strongest scent, and, as the dogs learned to work, weaker scents, such as heroin, were introduced. To give your dog the best chance of success, don't use your own scent; use something new and distinctive.

How to scent an article

Place some of your chosen scent – catnip, say – into a small bag, such as an organza jewellery pouch, one of the tiny plastic bags you find in stationery stores, or even a pouch made out of the foot of a pair of tights. The amount of scent you add to the bag depends on the size of the storage tin. For example, a large tin that had contained chocolates would take a bag containing a couple of tablespoons of scent, whereas an official TDS starter kit tin would need only a couple of teaspoons of bagged scent. Place the bag of scent into the tin alongside your unscented material articles, be they a mouse, pencil case or fleece tuggy.

Close the lid of the storage tin and leave for 24 hours. If you want to scent the article more quickly, use more catnip, and perhaps a second bag of scent on top of the articles in the tin so that the scent permeates from above and below. Leaving the tin on a sunny windowsill or in a warm area will help as the heat will animate the scent so that it is absorbed more quickly.

After a day, your material articles will be scented with catnip and ready to use for scentwork searches. Using something like catnip means that you will usually be able to smell it, too (although some can't).

Remember the rule: if you can smell it, you dog definitely can; if you can't, he probably can. When beginning scentwork, dispel any doubt about whether or not the article is scented. If you can smell it, perfect; if you're not sure whether or not the article has been in the tin long enough, leave it for longer. Asking your dog to locate something by scent requires you to make doubly sure that the article smells of the chosen scent. I recommend that you scent several articles so that you always have one ready to use. The bags of scent should last for around a couple of months, but do ensure that the catnip does not get damp as it will begin to rot and smell different (and bad!) If you and your dog are regularly scenting and searching for articles, simply replace the old catnip with a fresh supply every few months, and you're ready to go again.

Once you have used a scented article in

a search, do not return it to the storage tin immediately, but, instead, place it in a ziplock bag or alternative container until you can wash it. Putting it back in the tin when it is used and soggy will contaminate the tin, and everything that's in it, with the smell of your dog's slobber, and make the catnip damp. Do not store used articles in an area that you may want your dog to search, either, as it will become contaminated with their scent. I put mine on the windowsill of a room that I never ask my dogs to search (my kitchen), where they cannot reach them.

When you have a few used articles saved up, wash them in a 60°C/140°F cycle to help minimize the smell of the catnip and eliminate bacteria. Washing will not completely eliminate the smell of catnip/other scent, but will get rid of any other contamination. Don't use heavily-scented washing powder or a fabric conditioner, or the article will smell of these, which could confuse your dog. Scent-free powder for sensitive skin, or using just a tiny amount of your regular powder should be fine. It has been suggested that washing at a high temperature without any washing powder will clean and de-scent the article, but as my washing machine takes an age to wash at high temperatures I haven't tried this. If you have only a few articles to wash, you can do so using boiling water. Firstly, hand wash the articles in warm water containing a drop of washing power/liquid. Rinse, then place the articles in a bowl of boiling water, taking care to use an implement of some kind, rather than your hands, to fully submerge the articles. Soak for a few minutes; then carefully pour away the boiling water and thoroughly rinse the clean articles under the cold tap, before placing them on the dish rack or a radiator to dry.

Once dry, re-scent the article(s) as previously. I don't recommend drying the articles in a tumble dryer as they may contaminate the machine with their scent: ie everything you put in afterwards will carry a faint whiff of catnip, enough for your dog to detect.

Visit Hubble and Hattie on the web: www.hubbleandhattie.com
hubbleandhattie.blogspot.co.uk
• Details of all books • Special offers • Newsletter • New book news

Scentwork skills

Before you start

THERE ARE two main categories of response that your dog can give to tell you he has found something: active and passive.

Indications

Active indications are when a dog tries to access the scented article; in many cases, he will go into the 'hide,' be this a box or small area (behind a chair, say), to retrieve the article. This tactic is particularly useful in helping identify the specific hide rather than a general area.

A passive indication is a learned response, taught by the handler, whereby the dog stops and stares/sits when he locates a scent.

In my day, all Customs dogs gave active indications: they tried to get to the scent, showing me very clearly where the drugs were stashed. My job as handler, was to ensure that my dog got as close as possible to the drugs, but never came into contact with them; his safety was my prime concern at all times. I set up searches in which he could safely get to the training aid that contained the controlled

substance we were searching for, and gleefully rip it out of its hiding place in order to play with it. The skill was in making training aids that were strong enough to withstand rough play, gave easy access for me to remove the drugs during the reward game, but did not allow my dog to access these at any stage.

Happily, you won't need to learn this skill as you won't be asking your dog to search for anything that could pose a danger to him.

Currently, the Border Agency and Customs use dogs taught to give only a passive stare indication. Passive indication dogs began to be employed in Customs just before I left, and were used to search passengers.

For example, I might be asked to search a plane with my proactive dog whilst my colleague searched the plane's passengers with her passive dog.

Passive dogs allow teams to search without coming into contact with whatever they are searching (people), and without touching the source of the scent (explosives). The detection of firearms and explosives was, and, in many areas still is, done with passive indication

Flynn makes it very clear where the article is hidden ...

... and wastes no time going in to retrieve it!

dogs: it's obviously not safe for a dog to dig at a land mine or retrieve a gun.

But this style of searching has many more uses besides.

As previously mentioned, people can be searched for multiple scents, including money, food, drugs and weapons, without being touched by dog or handler, and such articles can be located without destroying evidence. And air samples from containers can be searched in seconds rather than the hours it would take to search the actual containers. Hence, Customs and other organisations can now use one dog to locate a variety of scents, such as currency or drugs, in a variety of areas, whether on a person or in a postal sack.

There are some downsides to passive indications. The trainer needs to be skilled in teaching a strong, reliable indication, and the handler needs to remain vigilant to maintain the training in order to preclude the dog from giving false indications. This is an issue because, on indicating, the dog is instantly rewarded, and, as a smart dog will figure out that when he sits he gets his reward, he may try sitting without actually finding the scent!

I think back to house-training a puppy. Every time the pup went near the back door I let him out, just in case he needed to toilet. There came a time when I had to determine whether he actually *did* need to toilet or simply wanted to go out and play. I made a judgement call: if I was wrong I found out fast as the puppy peed on the carpet; if I was right, he didn't.

Operationally, the detector dog handler cannot do this: she needs to trust her dog implicitly. However, not finding drugs on a person, for example, does not mean the dog has given a false indication, as the individual could have taken drugs, or might have been around others who were smoking drugs, which the dog can scent on his body or clothes. The only way to test whether a dog is giving good, positive indications is through training searches and simulated situations.

When I was operational, whenever we heard of fellow Customs officers taking a domestic flight, we would give them a packet containing a controlled substance to hide on their person or in their bags, for us to find with the dogs when they touched down at the airport. Training had to be this rigorous and real to ensure that our dogs were doing the best possible job. Without continuous training and testing, false indications can quickly creep into the dog's repertoire. This issue is exclusive to passive dogs because the passive dog receives an external reward provided by the handler, whereas the active dog's reward comes directly from the article he finds, which he can access himself.

Training a passive indication is a complex and challenging exercise involving chaining together a series of behaviours. Many trainers love this challenge as they can map out a training plan, work through clear steps, and end up with a dog who has an impressive skill.

And, of course, all dogs will at some point give passive responses. Those animals who have been taught active indications, where the objective is to get as close as possible to the scent source, will find themselves in situations where they simply cannot access the source,

because it's too high; too deep; too tight. In these cases, having been taught to get as close as they can, the dogs usually indicate where the article is by staring at the area, and sometimes by sitting (a common response when the article is high up). They are so precise that the handler can put their hand exactly on the spot that the dog is staring at and locate the article. This untrained passive response is a natural reaction to finding the scent source but not being able to physically access it. The dog remains entirely focused on the find and the anticipation of accessing it.

In instances where a dog cannot access the article, his reward will be to play with a ball thrown by his handler. The dog has no control of the reward, unlike the active indication where he can usually (in the early stages of training) reach the reward without relying on the handler. Missed observations that the dog has found the scent, mistiming with tossing the ball, and poor aim in this respect are not a concern when the dog is allowed to give an active indication.

The reward smells, or tastes (or both) of the scent. The connection between the scent and the reward is reinforced every time the dog finds the article. Having a separate unscented reward, such as a ball, adds an additional step to the search. In effect, the dog needs to find the scent in order to get the ball: the focus is on getting the ball; finding the scent is the means by which he gets it.

Once dogs have developed a strong, confident scentwork skill set, delays in reward and fewer rewards for finds, counter-balanced by the action of searching now being a reward in itself, are rarely an issue. But at the beginning, when learning the skill and building their experience, any barriers to rewards can be problematic.

The passive indication was developed for use by professional working dogs. Dogs specially and carefully selected by forces including the

army, air force, police and customs. These dogs must have strong motivation to play, a great desire to work, and possess stamina and concentration, both physical and mental.

Scentwork, as we practise it in Talking Dogs Scentwork®, is intended primarily as a fun activity for a dog, pitched and practised at a level that allows him to experience success and the joy of this, rather than as a detection tool. Dogs aren't 'selected' for the activity (for confidence or stamina, for example), so we don't exclude those who don't want to/ don't like, or feel comfortable about play, and, instead, provide an edible reward for them.

Active indications give all dogs the opportunity to participate, enjoy, and be rewarded, but to require all dogs to work in a set way is to exclude those who cannot adapt to a set structure, for whatever reason. All dogs can sniff out scents. The response to finding those scents is crucial in determining how much fun the dog is having; how rewarding he finds the experience, and how much he wants to do it again.

So, when deciding which indication to go with, consider the following criteria –

- Is the required indication designed to give you or your dog pleasure?

- Is your chosen indication a potential barrier or open door to a reward?

- Is your dog suited to the chosen indication?

- Do you have the skills to teach the chosen indication (practical as well as theory)?

- Are you prepared to put in the time and practise to maintain specific behaviours?

For the reasons discussed above, this manual deals with active indications and untrained passive indications.

Identifying common indications

When teaching an active indication, look for and identify those untrained, involuntary changes in your dog's body language that tell you he has found the scent. You will already be aware of changes in your dog's behaviour and demeanour when comes across certain everyday scents: when he is sniffing where another dog has urinated, for example, or when he is about to drop his shoulder and roll in something smelly and disgusting (to us, not to him!). I was able to spot the difference in the body language of my detector dog when searching a butcher's baggage, for example, as his indication was slightly different. Of course, had there been drugs in the bag, too, my dog would have given his usual drug indication (hiding contraband or controlled substances in food is a common tactic used by criminals). But this is a great way to help dogs find the article as anything that has a strong odour will carry the scent of the contraband with it, so will actually aid the dog in detecting the scent.

Common behaviour/body language changes that indicate a dog has found the scent include –

- His body becomes more rigid with a fixed focus. (Note: This is the one universal indication that I have observed with all dogs. Look for tension particularly across the shoulders, and a physical focus pointing towards the scent source)

- The check step – he suddenly goes back to double-check an area or article he has already passed

- He closes his mouth – this allows him to use his nose more effectively, ensuring that all of the scent hits the very best scent receptors in his nose

- He changes speed – some dogs, Spaniels,

for example - speed up and work faster; others, such as Rottweilers, slow down as they recognise the scent

- His tail position changes - the tail can become vertical, drop, wag very quickly or slow right down

- Further investigation - he lingers at the same spot as if checking it more thoroughly than other areas he has already passed. Quite often he will move on to another area, but return to this spot, as if comparing them in order to narrow the scent picture and pinpoint the find

- *Bisto Kid* - he starts air-scenting, as if following an invisible trail - just like the kids in the old "Ahh, Bisto" advert!

Your dog may show all of these indications, and a whole lot more besides. Observe them carefully and learn what they mean, as these are the clues that he is picking up in order to solve the puzzle you've set him. When you first begin scentwork with your dog, it can be difficult to spot these sometimes subtle signals. A solution for this is to video the searches and then watch them at your leisure so that you have time to rewind, repeat and review the recording.

Handling skills

One of the absolute joys of scentwork is that the dog takes the lead when it comes to following the scent. The handler is there to support him, and ensure that the search is efficient and thorough, but must at all times work to the dog's agenda. Even when we know where the article is hidden, we cannot know where the scent picture begins or ends. If we try to call our dog away from the scent picture and over to the article, we reduce his need to search. More importantly, calling him away

from the scent will confuse him, and may dent his confidence. If he's not indicating where we think he should be, and we move him away from the scent picture, he may become unsure of what we want him to do. I have seen strong, reliable dogs crumble within one search when called away from a scent. So we work with him, keeping enough distance between him and us so that we can see what he's doing but not impede his progress.

When he starts to indicate, give him space and support. Ask him if he's found something (the 'question': more of which later), but give him time to investigate. Stay back; don't crowd him. Let him make the decision about whether or not he's onto the scent. Get used to walking backwards so that you aren't looking the other way when he indicates, and are always ready to gesture to the next possible hiding place should he need your encouragement or assistance. In very hazardous areas, such as woodland, or during directed, linear searches that involve vehicles or people, walking backwards is not always necessary, or safe. But by the stage that he is carrying out more challenging searches such as these, your dog should be working confidently and you should be well-practiced at spotting his indications.

Quickly scan the area while doing your safety check (see page 33) before the search begins to identify any hazards, such as low beams, dips or bumps in the ground/floor, or furniture that you could bump into. Use your peripheral vision during the search to prevent you from tripping over or colliding into things that could distract the dog and hurt you. Ideally, you want to move lightly, quietly and swiftly to avoid distracting your dog, matching your pace to his, though not so slowly that he is kept waiting for something to do. Inexperienced dogs generally do not carry on searching under their own initiative (this will come later), so if you are not ready to suggest to him an area or article to investigate, the

Open hand gesture.
(Courtesy Bob Atkins/Your Dog Magazine)

Open hand gesture when searching for cheese. (Courtesy Bob Atkins/Your Dog Magazine)

flow of the search will be interrupted whilst he waits for you to decide, which can result in an energy drop – and a frustrated dog. Conversely, if you go too fast and hurry your dog, he won't have time to search properly, so find a balance; wait for him to look up or towards you before you cue the next area. If you have a really speedy dog, do not worry. You won't have to run around after him if you position yourself well. Head for the middle of the search area to allow easy access to all areas in plenty of time. As your dog becomes more experienced and the searches become more challenging, he will naturally slow down.

❶ Use a hand gesture to give your dog direction, and suggest areas and places that might contain the article. Actually moving toward certain areas, reinforced by a hand gesture, is key to convincing your dog that he should work with you rather than on his own. He needs to know you can be of assistance, and the key here is *assistance* rather than control. ❷ The hand gesture should be fluid and fleeting, and using the whole arm rather than just a hand gives a clearer signal. Simply pointing at areas to search is not clear enough, and may encourage the dog to look at your hand rather than in the direction you want him to. ❸

Specifically, the hand gesture should be like that used when showing someone to a seat, moving fluidly, with grace and purpose,

Don't point! (Courtesy Bob Atkins/Your Dog Magazine)

and not stiff and inflexible. Make it a natural movement to show your dog the area or article you'd like him to search, then move on.

When working your dog at height, or if asking him to jump up onto things such as tables, chairs, benches, unsteady mounds, etc, I recommend that he wear a harness.

There are many harnesses on the market, but go for a well-fitted, comfortable and supportive example that you can securely grasp the back off to take his weight as he jumps off things, and be ready to support him as he jumps up onto things. The classic Karenswood Breast Harness is a good choice as it's simple and strong (see the resources page for more details). ❹

Use a harness to support your dog as he jumps on and off objects.
(Courtesy Bob Atkins/Your Dog Magazine)

My harness of choice, and the one currently used by the Border Agency and Customs, is the Catac Working Dog Harness, which has a broad girth strap that gives good support, and, as it is made of strong, flexible webbing, will not stretch or snap: always a worry with leather harnesses.

The harness should fit well, and should not have raised handles or other protruding parts that could become caught or snagged during a search. It should not tighten or restrict your dog's movement when pressure is applied, so no-pull harnesses (those with moving parts) are a definite no-no for scentwork. Go for wide webbing, quality materials, and good fit.

You should not use the harness to lift your dog, but to support him as he jumps up onto slippery or unsteady surfaces, and to take the strain as he jumps down. Many detector dogs are retired due to arthritis in the elbows and shoulders – a result of repeated unsupported landings. Get used to automatically putting your hand under the top of the harness, in readiness to take the strain, but without applying any pressure.

Understandably, many dogs dislike being pulled or lifted by harnesses, and, based on previous experience, can stop working or pull away when the handler touches the harness. Practise following your dog, letting him move freely while your hand remains on the harness. If you use a light touch that doesn't impede his progress, he will learn that you are there to support and help him; not restrict and control him. This means that you have to anticipate where your dog will move to next in order to position yourself well, should you need to be close enough to physically support him, or far enough away to give him space to work the area.

A word of warning when using a harness: never hold the harness by the ring to which the lead is attached, as this can easily result in spiral fractures of your fingers if the dog turns unexpectedly. Always put your whole hand under the strap that goes across his back instead.

The method for moving your dog around the search area is surprisingly simple: you, the handler, simply move to wherever you want your dog to search. You don't have to say anything, call him over, or even point. Quiet, swift movement around the search area will encourage your dog to move. By moving backwards, you remain engaged with the dog and you'll have strong teamwork. Play on your dog's curiosity. He will wonder why you've moved to a specific area, so will move towards you to see what's there. Using this simple technique you can cover the entire search area.

Handler movement moves the dog.
(Courtesy Wayne Holt)

Always plan ahead, thinking about where to go next; ensuring that nothing in the search area is missed or repeatedly searched. Don't become sidelined or cornered: work from inside the area, otherwise you may become stuck, and will interrupt the flow, making it difficult to follow the search patterns. Should this happen, potential hiding places could be missed, and the area would not be thoroughly searched. And, quite often, you will draw your dog outside the search area. This can be counter-intuitive to handlers who have competed with their dog in activities such as Working Trials, as very often they do remain outside the search area, and send in their dog to work alone.

To complement your handling skills, use your voice (again, some handlers will not be used to doing this, mid-search). To begin a search, decide on a word or words that mean 'Go find something using your nose.' When I was in Customs, our search word was 'fetch,' but as this is very often used in connection with a 'seen' retrieve (a dog is sent to bring back an object he's seen being thrown), it's better to use another cue to send your dog to search for an unseen article. I use 'find it!' Other cues you could use include 'seek,' 'search' or 'scent.' With my dogs, I use 'fetch' if they are searching with their eyes, and 'find it' when searching with their nose. It doesn't matter which cue you choose as long as it's not one you already use to mean something else.

If you already play scent games with your dogs – hunting for their toys around the house, or searching for treats in the garden – you can use the same search word to cue this game. As long as you are asking your dog to search using his nose, this is absolutely fine. A cue is important, as this lets your dog know that the scentwork game is on. No cue means it's not on. Dogs so enjoy scentwork they want to do it all the time, so to make it even clearer

Bridget has bells attached to her harness so she knows it's time to go to work.

when this is going to happen, use a specific harness or collar for scentwork games only. Some handlers even attach bells to their dog's harness as an aural cue to scentwork fun.

Give the 'find it' cue at the start of the search, as you release or take your dog into the search area, and only repeat it if your dog asks for help: when he looks over to you, or seems to be losing track of the task in hand. Apart from that, stay quiet and let your dog work. Watch, move, and work with him: it's a dance; you are his partner.

Let your dog know when he's doing well – a well-timed 'good lad,' 'clever girl' or 'nice' the first time he puts his head inside a box, or jumps onto a table, sniffs into a metal bucket or paws at a box to flip it over, let's him know he's on the right track, and you are there to support him. And that means he's likely to do it again, which is exactly what you want. You want him to know you like it when he pushes into boxes or touches articles that are unfamiliar, or is brave enough to jump onto something unsteady. Total silence when he's learning can be unnerving, giving rise to uncertainty and knocking his confidence, whereas a warm,

Asking the question. (Courtesy Bob Atkins/Your Dog Magazine)

verbal reward can encourage curiosity and inspire bravery. So be kind, be supportive, and be thoughtful when you speak.

In the next section you will discover two particular circumstances when you most definitely need to speak: the 'question' and the 'drive-in.'

How to respond to an indication

When you see changes in your dog's behaviour, ask him a question: 'Have you found something?' or 'Where is it?' This is an acknowledgement to him that you have noticed the change, and encourages him to investigate the scent picture he's located. It may be that, on further investigation, he finds nothing there and moves on; that's fine: he can 'see' the picture; you can't. Even if you know the article is right there, remember that the scent may be flowing from another direction.

If you ask the question and your dog becomes more intense, more determined, continue to encourage him to work towards the find. 'Where is it?'/'Have you got something?'/'What've you got, then?' are all examples of how to keep him working, following the scent in order to lead you directly to the source. Don't tell him 'Find it, find it' because he has already found it. He's onto the scent; now he's trailing it back to source.

Step away as you ask the question to allow your dog to answer 'yes' or 'no.'

When you ask the question, you must allow your dog to answer 'yes' or 'no.' If you are doing a blind search, you will have no idea where the article is hidden, and, even if you *do* know, you don't know to where the scent has moved. Therefore, you don't know the answer to the question.

So how can your dog answer? As you ask the question, step right away from him. This can very difficult to do at first, because you will be just as keen as him to see if he has got it right, but if you step towards your dog, he may take this as a sign that you know where the article is hidden, and that you are stepping towards it. He can become more

excited as a result, which you may mistake for further or stronger indications that he's has found the article, and therefore move closer still. Ultimately, you each convince the other that you know where the article is hidden, and end up disappointed and confused when it isn't where you expect it to be! So, ask the question ... and step away.

Interestingly, stepping away whilst asking the question is unlikely to draw your dog from the scent picture. Moving around an area has the desired effect of drawing your dog into that space, but asking the question as you move away will elicit a different response.

If he's hit the scent, he will want to stay

with it. Walking backwards helps greatly in this objective, because you can move away from your dog whilst remaining engaged with him. If he has not found the scent and the answer to your question is 'no,' he will move away with you.

When that happens, use the hand gesture to suggest somewhere else for him to search and continue on. Moving right back, away from your dog as you ask the question, not only allows him to investigate without feeling pressured, but also lets you see all of him and all of his indications, and gives him access to a large area in order to track the scent. It's all too easy to inadvertently block your dog from the scent source with your own body. By moving back at least four or five paces, you give him unfettered access to a bigger area, while still remaining engaged with him.

Asking the question should not be used as a diagnostic tool to help you figure out if your dog is actually indicating, but to prompt him to work towards the scent source or move on to work in another part of the search area. Feel free to ask the question several times during the search, but only when you think you are seeing indications. The more you search, the more you will be able to distinguish between indications and interest. Interest is when the dog is fluid, on the move, checking things out. Indications are when he becomes more intense; more focused; more specific.

Once you know he has hit the scent, encourage your dog to work right to the source. Stand back and give him the space to work it out, because if you move in too fast, he will retreat to let you look. Nothing builds his confidence like locating and retrieving the article himself. You are there to give support and provide assistance, should he really need it, but his job is not complete until he pinpoints the article.

If he needs to push something out of the way, rip something, find a direct route or stand

on something to access the hide, you can start the 'drive-in,' an escalating commentary that encourages your dog to go for it, given in a tone that begins as questioning and gradually builds in excitement and encouragement, peaking when he pinpoints the article. 'Go on, then. You find it. You get it. Good lad. Well done. Good boy!'

Be ready to pull back with the drive-in or maintain it for a longer period at a steady but always encouraging tone. I have had to do this for minutes at a time ... that doesn't sound very long, but give it a try (without your dog): it can be tricky. You don't want to peak too soon, or turn the drive-in into a nag or a distraction. You have to pitch it just right: when you do, it can be a valuable asset.

Handling tips
Holding the lead
You will need both hands to search, and a lead will get in the way, so stow it in your pocket or leave it outside the search area before you begin. Leaving it in the search area could be distracting for your dog, and a trip hazard for you.

Following your dog
Ask yourself: 'How does following my dog assist the search?' Following means you are always behind the action, reacting rather than anticipating. Instead, stay in front of your dog to keep the search flowing, and provide him with lots of places to look next, allowing him to take the lead when it comes to following a scent he has picked up.

Not asking the question
The question helps a dog re-examine the area, and allows him to tell you no, it's not the scent he's looking for, or yes, that smells good. It can help strengthen the indication, and encourages your dog if he's unsure of what he's smelling. Without the question, your

dog is unsupported: he has no way of knowing that you have observed his body language change. And remember, if you step back without asking the question, you are actually drawing your dog away from where the article is possibly hidden.

Not moving away when asking the question

If you stay where you are, or, even worse, move towards your dog when asking the question, you can skew his answer. Your dog must be able to reply 'yes' or 'no' to the question, so if you stay where you are, you don't give him the opportunity to move away from an incorrect scent. If you move towards your dog, there's a good chance that he will think you know where the article is hidden: very confusing for him if it isn't actually there.

And if it *is* there, your dog will simply stop searching, safe in the knowledge that you are doing so!

Getting in the way of your dog

Staying too close to your dog whilst he searches will inevitably result in you getting in his way, blocking his route, interrupting the flow of the search, and even inadvertently blocking him from accessing the article.

Most dogs – and people – dislike being crowded, so will put more effort into moving away from you to create space than they will into searching the area.

Not covering the whole area/getting stuck in one spot

It is very easy to simply come to a halt, or move about in only one section of the search area, and so neglect other parts; this happens most often if you follow behind your dog.

Instead, try walking backwards in front of him, as this helps to highlight where you'd like him to search, and results in a more thorough and efficient search. Keep moving so that you cover the whole area, giving your dog access to everything.

This issue becomes less of a problem once you have a search plan: ie learnt the search patterns.

Safety check

Before using a search area, get into the habit of performing a safety check for hazards that could be dangerous to you and your dog.

On an operational search, the dog handler would be the first, and only, person to go into the area to be searched, as lots of people in the area moving things around causes air disturbance, and makes it more difficult for the dog to detect target scents: he is still likely to find whatever might be there, but will take longer and therefore be less efficient.

The handler must check for needles, glass; look for moving parts in machinery, or pallets of boxes not safely stacked. Only once the handler is satisfied that the area is safe for the dog would she begin the search.

Common hazards to look out for/avoid include –

• Cables and flexes hanging from computers, lamps, etc. We see these every day but are unlikely to really notice them

• Electrical sockets – must not be searched by companion dogs: do not put your dog's wet nose anywhere near these. As an additional safety measure, turn off switches, and, ideally, insert socket protectors

• Hot areas such as radiators, fires, exhaust pipes, ovens, etc

• Slippery surfaces – at ground level and on tables and higher surfaces. Also check the stability before asking your dog to jump onto something

- Toxic or hazardous substances such as bleach, petrol, cleaning products, oil (commonly found in the kitchen, bathroom, sheds and garages)

- Sharp edges (rubbish, tin cans, etc)

- Broken glass on the ground or in or around cars

- Holes in the ground or loose rubble that you could slip on or your dog could get caught in

- Food (not so much a hazard as a distraction, but worth removing before the search begins)

Decide what to do about any hazards you identify. Maybe you can make them safe by laying them down, making them steady, or removing them from the area. Where they cannot be made safe, decide whether to still search the area and avoid the hazard, or not search the area at all.

If you decide on the former, take great care when directing your dog during the search to ensure that he follows your cues to avoid the hazard. Sometimes, having a helper stand in front of the hazard can be useful; other times, use your own body to block it while gesturing towards a safer area.

Hiding the article

Hiding the article is a skill in itself. The hiding place always has to be appropriate to the dog doing the search. Sometimes, it has to be appropriate to you if working on your own handling skills rather than your dog's searching ability.

For example, if you're having trouble identifying your dog's indications and having time to react, a longer search with a 'deeper' hide can be very useful.

A classic example of a deeper hide is when an article – such as a soft toy saturated with the scent of catnip – is concealed inside several boxes, but is emitting a good, strong odour, and is hidden where the dog cannot immediately gain access to it, which ensures that your dog will give a bigger indication. The scent is still strong, but your dog will remain at the hide for longer as he physically works at retrieving the article through the layers of multiple boxes. This extra time will allow you to spot the indication, ask the question, and encourage your dog to get in there and retrieve the article.

Ascertain that the article will fit/remain in its hiding place before you actually locate it to avoid contaminating the area. Use your right hand (which you use to guide your dog and suggest places for him to look, so the one that should always remain uncontaminated by the scent) to test the space and determine if the article will fit, while holding the scented article in your left.

You can make items easier – or harder – to locate by disturbing the airflow around the hide. If you have a room full of boxes but only one box has been moved, the airflow around that box will have been disturbed, which your dog will detect and be drawn to. Moving several boxes will create additional airflow disturbance, making the search more difficult and realistic, as your dog must ensure he detects the scent *within* the disturbance rather than just the disturbance.

You can build on this by disturbing multiple objects in the area: move several boxes and shake a few curtains, for example, or move a few cushions, chairs, plant pots (depending on where you are working). Obviously, you must not contaminate what you touch with the scent you want your dog to find.

Just as you can use disturbance to create more of a challenge, so you can use it to help your dog if he is uncertain. As previously mentioned, disturbing only the box containing the article highlights that particular box, drawing your dog to it and the article. I don't recommend you use this tactic on a regular basis, however, as we want the dog to identify the scent rather than the disturbance. But used carefully and occasionally, this ploy can help boost confidence.

Some areas could be described as self-disturbing: where there is airflow from open windows; heaters pumping out hot air; moving parts in engine rooms, and searches done outside. Weather plays havoc with scent pictures, diluting them, dispersing them, and sending the scent in the opposite direction to the hide, which is why they are more difficult than inside searches, where the environment is much more easily controlled. Hence why I prefer to start scentwork indoors. Always set up your dog to succeed.

Once you have hidden the article, don't leave the storage tin or used articles in the search area, or even close to it, as your dog will find them and then have to be worked away from them, adding unnecessary extra time and effort to the search. Similarly, don't open the storage box inside the search area as this will allow the scent to spill out of the tin, contaminating wherever you are in the search area. Instead, open the tin to remove the article *outside* the search area.

Practicalities

When using the same area to conduct multiple searches, make a note of where you have hidden the article each time so that you know when your dog is indicating on a previous hide. Acknowledge the indication ('Good lad'), then help him move on to continue the search. Don't ignore or reprimand your dog for indicating on previous hides: a warm acknowledgement lets him know you like what he's done, and now you'd like him to continue on to find a scent somewhere else.

Taking notes will also help you keep track of where you hide articles so that you both make progress, and are not just using the same or similar locations.

For advanced dogs, placing a new article in a previous hide is a real test of the handler's skills in reading their dog.

Using cardboard boxes

Anyone who has been to my workshops or watched my DVDs will know that I often use cardboard boxes as hides, especially in the early stages of scentwork. This is purely for practical reasons.

Most scentwork workshops are conducted in halls that contain very little except chairs and a few tables, so I therefore need something in which to hide the article. I know that some methods of teaching companion dogs scentwork place particular emphasis on boxes, but I do not, and if you are reading this manual and want to start your dog searching at home, there's no need to clutter your house with dozens of cardboard boxes. An average home already has lots of things that you can use: tables, chairs, bookcases, beds, storage, rugs, and much more besides. I use boxes simply to utilise the space in the middle of the room, and to allow a dog to smell but not see the article. If you are running out of places to hide things, then, of course, use boxes.

Warning!

Many scentwork folk develop what some might call a hoarding habit! Others (like me) call it 'collecting essential equipment.' Spotting a box with drawers or multiple sections, or an unusual container or toy (both of which I can use in scentwork) makes me happier than the best chocolate cake!

Box material/quality

If using boxes, consider the material/quality, size and previous contents of them.

Krumble gives this box a good sniff!

Not all cardboard is created equal. You will know this if you have flattened boxes for recycling. Some squash in a second; others you have to jump on to flatten. The difference is the thickness of the cardboard.

Some very rigid boxes are made of several layers of flat and/or corrugated cardboard. The thicker and more rigid the cardboard, the harder it is for the scent to pass through, because the cardboard fibres are closer together, and there are more layers for the air and scent to negotiate their way through.

Thin, cheap cardboard is the opposite, and will quickly become saturated with scent. This means that the box will begin to smell of the scented article, and, rather than simply holding the scented air inside it (which your dog can best access via any gaps in the cardboard, rather than on the cardboard itself), the smell will seep out, giving the dog more opportunities to detect the source. This is more easily seen when using cheese as the scent. Cheese is fatty, and when it is stuck onto cardboard it leaves a grease mark. Scented articles do the same thing; it's just that we can't see it.

Additional layers of paper or card applied

on top of the cardboard will also hinder scent movement. Many boxes have printed covers applied on top of the cardboard.

The basic rule is that the glossier the outside of the box, the tougher it is for scent to pass through. So challenging boxes in which to hide articles include very thick, rigid, glossy ones that have contained computers or electrical appliances. Good starter boxes are those made of plain, thin, brown cardboard.

Size matters!

During starter searches, the size of the box must be defined by the size of dog. If your dog can't reach the article in the box without tipping it over or jumping into it, then the box is too big. And it's too deep if he has to get all the way inside to retrieve the article.

Avoid these situations in the initial stages of scentwork. They can be introduced as extra challenges later, or for dogs who have few body contact issues, and couldn't care less if the box touches their side or head, or tips over when they try to get inside it.

You want to set up your dog to be successful, build his confidence, and have fun retrieving the article. If you have to help him retrieve it at the beginning of his scentwork journey, he may come to rely on you to always do this, rather than only when the article is completely inaccessible.

A bigger box may also dilute the scent more as it travels around a larger area inside, but does create a bigger scent picture (assuming there is flow from inside to outside the box). Obviously, a small box allows for less dilution but creates a smaller scent picture. However, unless you are comparing a box that contained a fridge freezer with a matchbox, in most situations this makes little difference,

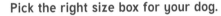

Pick the right size box for your dog.

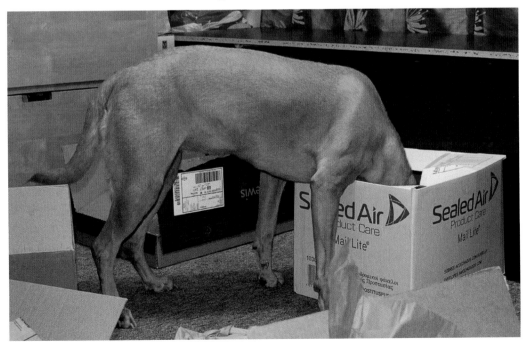

although it's always good to know what the scent is likely to be doing in the hide.

Previous contents

Whatever was in the box previously will have left its scent inside, and in the cardboard. As scents can come from inside and outside the box, it will also smell of where it's been stored.

The smell of foodstuffs, both human and animal, can confuse your dog, drawing him over to the box that smells of food, and away from the box that smells of catnip. In the later stages of scentwork this is fine, but it can cause dilemmas for the starter scentworker.

Avoid using boxes that contained cereal, dog food, cat food, veterinary medicines (the outside is likely to smell of the veterinary practice, and/or of animals), and boxes that have been stored in areas where real mice or other creatures could have contaminated them (such as sheds or garages).

How to use

The final consideration is how to use the boxes. You have so many choices: let's split them into 'easier' and 'more challenging' configurations.

Easier

• The box could be open and upright, or open and on its side, and facing towards your dog as he enters the search area (easier than facing away). Even closing one flap of the box doesn't make it too hard, as there's still good access to the scent, even though the article is shielded from sight

• Tip the box and balance it along the edge of another box (only do this if your dog won't be spooked by the box moving or falling off the other box)

• Align the open end of one box against another to give a slightly more challenging

search. Shoe boxes with lids are excellent for this, and can be placed in all sorts of configurations to allow more or less air to flow out

• Boxes with non-detachable lids can be placed upside down so that the article is actually lying on the floor rather than in the box. The boxes won't lie flat, because of the lid, so the scent moves freely through both sides of the hide. These hides are great for dogs who need help in moving the box to access the find. A quick nudge will expose the article, and your dog immediately learns that moving the box can be easy and rewarding.

Have a play; see what works best for your dog.

More challenging

• Close all of the box flaps

• Hide boxes inside other, bigger boxes

• Turn the box upside down, flat against the floor, flaps open, so that the article is again on the floor (this is different to the exercise with a box with a non-detachable lid because, in this case, the scent in trapped under the box rather than being able to flow out through the gap created by the lid

• Placing the box containing the article at the very edge, or in the corner of, a search area can be more of a challenge as it can be more easily missed

• A box placed in the middle of a search area is often missed, should the handler inadvertently block access to it, or forget to ask the dog to search here

• Cheese squashed into the corners of a box

How you lay out the boxes determines the challenge of the search.

Cherry searches the boxes in this small space.

or under the flaps, so that the box appears empty, are crafty hides. I like that the dog has first to identify the box, and then do a second mini search to locate the cheese on/in it, and that, when the handler looks inside (instead of trusting their dog), it appears that the box is empty

• Squashing cheese in the bottom corners

of an upside down box works well, as most dogs hit the scent from the outside. The fat of the cheese soaks into the cardboard, and the corner join allows air to escape, making this a nice hide. This one is in the more challenging section because, even though the dog can smell the cheese, he cannot access it without help, unless he is particularly confident and creative, in which case, he'll flip over the box or chew through it!

Once you have used a cardboard box to hide food, it should not be used again as your dog's saliva will have contaminated it when he found the previous food article.

A box that has been used to hide a non-food article, which has little or no canine contamination, can be used again, but only as the hide. Don't leave it empty in the search area as the beginner dog may indicate on it, and be confused that there is nothing to find inside. Instead, store it separately from unused boxes, and reuse it as a hiding place during a future search.

For practical reasons, at the end of a scentwork session, it's best to fold up used boxes and put them into the recycling bin. Having multiple storage areas for used and unused boxes gets complicated, and takes up double the space.

Additional tips

• Keep your hands clean so that when you are holding your dog's lead and guiding him, he doesn't pick up the scent from them

• Use (ideally) unscented antibacterial hand cleaners or baby wipes, ensuring these are kept away from your dog. Remember, though, that nothing beats good old-fashioned soap and water

- If you want to be even more careful to avoid contamination, wear disposable rubber gloves when handling scented articles. It is extremely easy to cross-contaminate scents, and this helps reduce that risk. You can also use tongs if you don't want to touch the article at all. However, dogs are extremely good at working, despite mild contamination in the area, so all is not lost if you forget

- When practicing or working, remember where you've hidden the articles, and, if scented, what the scent is. Your dog may appear to give 'false' indications (indicates he has found something but there is nothing there), which may be because he can still smell an article from a previous search. Acknowledge his indication ('Good lad'), and move him on to continue searching the area. Dogs using active indications do not give false indications – there's no benefit to them in doing that (as previously explained)

- If the weather or environment is hot, your dog will pant more. Panting and sniffing are mutually(ish) exclusive, so perform searches before hard exercise, or in the cool of the morning rather than the heat of the afternoon

- Look after your dog's welfare before and after searches. Make sure he has a chance to go to the toilet and have a drink before starting to search, and give him access to water at all times during and following searches

- Give your dog a chance to rest between searches – scentwork is fun but also hard work. Offer him a drink of water and put him into a settle, or back into the car or his crate

- As your dog hones his skills, ask other people to hide articles: if you always know where the article is, you can miss indications, try to override your dog, and weaken the teamwork between you. Not knowing where the article is hidden is known as a 'blind' search

Ensure that water is available to your dog at all times.

(Courtesy Bob Atkins/Your Dog Magazine)

The Search

Search types

Free search

THE FREE search provides the first opportunity for your dog to scan the area to see if he can catch a whiff of the scented article. Free searching carries no restrictions: your dog can go high, low – anywhere he wants.

Some dogs work at a very fast pace, and will run around the search area, whilst others will wander around at a steady speed. Whatever the speed, as long as they're sniffing, they're working. Some dogs move from one side of the area to the other, in similar fashion to gundogs when they are quartering in a field. All have the same aim: to pick up the scent and work it back the source.

During the free search, the handler's job is to carefully observe their dog, keep out of his way, and subtly move him around the search area. Imagine you are the ball in a giant pinball game, bouncing off an invisible bubble that totally surrounds your dog, and sends you in the opposite direction to him. If he moves to the left, you move to the right; if he goes north, you go south.

This constant movement keeps the search energized and flowing, and encourages your dog to cover the whole area. He will naturally move towards you, so by positioning yourself in such a way that the entire search area can be accessed you can ensure your dog will move into those areas, too. In general, if you stay around 2m/6ft away from your dog you will be close enough to observe and assist, but far enough away to avoid hindering the search. Walk backwards while moving around, never taking your eyes off him, always ready to ask 'Have you got something?' Give encouragement if your dog gives something a good, investigative sniff, and remind him to keep working – by saying 'Find it' – should he look up or at you.

The free search helps a dog become familiar with each particular search area. He can figure out what he can jump on or go under, and where the boundaries are. It also gives him

time to settle into the search before he has to follow more challenging patterns.

Directed search

If you have completed the free search without locating the find, or if you know that there is more than one find, the next step is to begin the directed search – a key skill that's required in the majority of searches.

The directed search – as its name suggests – is a very specific and thorough search, whose purpose is to help the dog examine the entire area in detail, ensuring that he checks high, low, and everywhere in-between. Unlike the free search where the dog can move back and

Placing food for a directed search.
(Courtesy Bob Atkins/Your Dog Magazine)

Always be ahead of the action, whilst walking backwards. (Courtesy Wayne Holt)

forth between sections, the directed search entails dog and handler working together systematically along the area.

An example of this would be working along a stretch of wall in the living room, which might take in a skirting board, dado rail and radiator. You would guide your dog up to the dado, down to the skirting board, behind and around the radiator. As this is for fun, for reasons of safety I do not recommend searching

electrical sockets along the way. Place your guiding hand wherever you want your dog to put his nose: be very specific. As your dog's nose comes to meet your hand, move your hand to the next spot so that you are always moving; always in readiness to show him the next section.

To begin a directed search, place yourself directly in front of your dog, guiding with your right hand. If the search is done on-lead, hold this in your left hand. Walk backwards along the search area, almost using your body as a block to prevent your dog passing you, keeping close to where you are searching and facing your dog at all times. Leaving too much space between your side and the search area (the perimeter of a room, or a vehicle, say), provides an opportunity for your dog to rush forward and past you.

Ideally, you want to move your dog forward (remembering to walk backwards yourself) without having to go back and re-search a section. Backtracking interrupts the flow of the search and is inefficient, and constant interruptions can demotivate your dog, and erode his desire to work so closely with you.

way you came, with your dog in front of you, whereby you will be following your dog and unable to assist in any meaningful manner.

Working your dog on-lead can help focus his attention on one specific area, and prevents him from going too wide and covering areas not included in the search. The lead is used for when it would be unsafe for him to work off-lead, most especially during vehicle searches. On-lead searches are also used when searching people, in order to keep the dog safe from them, and them safe from the dog should they be frightened or nervous of dogs. Working on-lead also helps the novice handler learn how to maintain body position, and note the dog's indications at close range – which can be difficult. But, by asking the

Cherry and I carry out a directed search along the fence.
(Courtesy Bob Atkins/Your Dog Magazine)

However, should your dog hit the scent and want to move past you, step aside and allow him to do so. Make a mental note of where he broke off the directed search. If he indicates, ask the question 'Have you got something?', step back and get ready to help or drive him in to locate the find. If he does not indicate or moves away from the area when the question is asked, bring him back round to the spot where he broke off the directed search and resume searching. In this way, the search will flow and nothing should be missed.

In order to maintain the correct position – you walking backwards in a clockwise direction – always bring your dog round to your right so that you are between him and the area being searched, rather than walking back the

Lynn keeps the lead long and loose while watching Burt search the bags.

question: 'Have you got something?' and moving away as usual, it's possible to see more of your dog and so better interpret his behaviour.

The lead should be long enough to allow you to do this, and, in this respect, although a standard length lead is fine, a slightly longer one is better. Do not let the end of the lead dangle; hold it loosely in your hand and out of the way. Lead skills are definitely worth practicing: it's not intended to guide your dog; nor to regulate his speed, as any such interference will distract him from his work.

Should you want your dog to slow his pace, put out more articles for him to search. There is never any reason for him to go faster: slow, steady dogs search beautifully. If you ask him to go quicker than he would naturally do, it will put him off, and he will begin to miss finds. Reliability is what's required.

Some dogs need time to settle into a directed search, especially when they are learning, so choose a set area – one wall, say, or a line of chairs or boxes – and search just that. If he's too fast or unfocused at the start, let him do a free search along or around the area first, then bring him back to the starting point to carry out a thorough search.

I often find that handlers do not provide their dog with sufficient detail during directed searches. They skip things, concentrating only on the high or low areas instead of both, or make assumptions about where articles might be hidden, and don't ask their dog to search there. The intention is to be very thorough, so that, at the end of the search, the team can confidently conclude that the article has been found, or that there was nothing *to* find and the area is clear.

In being thorough, however, it's important to remember not to move so slowly that your dog becomes bored. Match your dog's pace in terms of speed and where he's sniffing, and stimulate his interest by showing him where to look.

Keep moving: the only time you should stop is when you are waiting for him to answer the question 'Have you got something? Be thorough; match your dog's pace; keep moving.

Blind search

In this situation the handler does not know where the hide is, and is working blind. Technically, this is a double blind search as neither handler nor dog knows where the hide is, but as the searches are always blind for the dog, I'll refer to this as a blind search.

The advantage of the blind search is that you must learn to identify your dog's indications, and rely on him to tell you where the find is. Make sure not to search for the article yourself when doing a blind search, but look for areas for your dog to search.

My preference when first starting out with TDS is to enlist the help of a friend so that you can carry out blind searches, as doing so is the fast track to learning your dog's indications and trusting him. Known searches – where you have hidden the article, or know where it has been hidden – mean you have to be extra sure that you are actually seeing an indication when your dog is close to the hide (to check for this, video your searches to review later). If you assume that your dog has indicated when he hasn't, this may preclude your dog from giving good indications as you have inadvertently been telling him where the article is!

Blind searches are essential when it comes to really working with and trusting your dog. In my workshops it is immediately apparent with some people that they have been hiding their own finds, because they do not recognize their dog's indications (which are often weaker than they'd like). This is often due to the handler letting their dog know that he's found the article by asking the question when he's only close to the find, rather than seeing him indicate that he has found it. Blind searches are the only way to truly allow your dog to indicate reliably and confidently.

Known search

This is the opposite of the blind search, as the handler knows where the hide is. You may have hidden the article yourself, for example, or been told where it is by your helper. Known searches are useful when you do not have a helper, or when you want to practise in specific areas, introduce new elements, or make it easier for your dog.

Treat known searches with caution and respect, as the downside is that they can encourage lazy handling, and give inadvertent cues to your dog about the location of the hide, thereby reducing the reliability of his indications. Carry out known searches sparingly and with care.

Blank search

During the early stages of scentwork, you will have very little time to practise your search patterns, as you will have designed these searches to be quick and easy for your dog. As your dog's skills grow it can be difficult to grow your own handling skills at the same rate, as, no matter how hard you try, your dog will locate the find too quickly.

The remedy to this is a blank search, in which an article is not pre-hidden in the search area. In other words, your dog searches an empty room, and when you're ready or the entire area has been covered, your helper puts out a quick, easy find as a reward for all his hard work. Don't assume that this is tricking your dog (which I am very much against). Everything is as it should be for your dog: the search is the same, just longer, and he gets a find at some point.

Before your scentwork session, advise your helper that you'd like to mix blank searches with some that have articles hidden before the search begins. In this instance, your helper should not tell you whether or not an article has been hidden, in order that the search is a thorough one. If you search as though there is something there, your dog will, too, but if you know that the search is a blank one, it can be all too easy to skip areas and not search as thoroughly, safe in the knowledge that you've not missed the find.

The blank search gives you time. Time to do the corners, the perimeter, the interior, and it teaches you to be thorough. Did your dog really *search* the corner or did he just wander over there? Hiding finds in corners will help ensure that dog and hander do the job properly.

Once the area has been cleared (you can confirm there is nothing to find) surreptitiously drop the article behind you, ideally tossing it behind a chair or object close by. (Often, these quick finds are called secondary aids, as they aid the search second time around.) Ideally, drop the scented article out of your left back pocket using your left hand, whilst guiding your dog around to the right using your right hand, in order to search the area again. This is not always easy, so a helper is an asset.

If you have a helper on hand, have them place the article as you approach the end of the search, taking care not to alert your dog to this twist in the game. The article doesn't need to be completely hidden, and nor should it be simply placed on the ground in the open: as long as your dog has to carry out a quick search to find it, that's fine. It's important to say that your dog does need to find the article himself, and not one that is tossed to him by you or your helper, as this is a sure-fire way to teach him that the finds will come from you and not from the search area.

You can put out a find at any point in a blank search, especially if your dog begins to become de-motivated or frustrated if he's worked too long without a find. For some dogs this could be after only a couple of minutes – especially if he's used to finding something within the first thirty seconds – for others, it could be when they've worked their socks off for ten minutes without finding anything.

Watch to see if your dog is looking at you more often than usual, appears to be losing confidence, or is beginning to pick up random articles. If any of these occur, look back at your search notes to check at roughly what point your dog has been hitting the finds, and carefully plan your search around this, priming your helper to toss in a reward find at just the right time. Ideally, the find needs to go out before your dog begins to show frustration or de-motivation: looking back at your notes will help you to predict when and where to place the articles.

Operationally, search dogs do not find contraband at each and every search, but will find a reward or two every day by using this technique. Once the handler has declared the area clear, he or she will often get a colleague to hide the article for them. On other days, when there is time to top up training, they will use much more difficult hides, perhaps practicing on a concealment similar to one found by a fellow dog team, or based on smuggling intelligence.

The blank search is what allows a dog to build the stamina and concentration required to search for the most challenging hides, and in the most taxing areas. At this stage in their work, the search itself has become almost as rewarding as the find, so they are more than happy to work for long periods without finding anything.

Blank searches also help the handler learn how to properly clear an area. With initial searches, the search stops once the article is found, but a blank search means that searches can go on for longer, and so become more thorough. Having the confidence to declare there are no hidden articles in an area is an important skill, as a handler must be sure they haven't missed anything, whilst still working efficiently and to the duration that their dog finds comfortable. Repeatedly searching the same area without a find can be tiring, puzzling and frustrating for a dog.

An interesting observation is that dogs do keep track of where they have already searched, and I have often witnessed animals either coming to a complete stop, or being reluctant to continue searching when asked to search the same area/article again and again. The dog knows that the area is clear, but the handler doesn't fully trust his instincts. A practical way to address this issue of over-searching the same area is to set a time limit on the search. That way, everything has to be searched efficiently and thoroughly the first time.

The search plan

When searching with your dog it's very easy to forget where you've been, what you've already searched, and what you've still to check (even though your dog may remember!). Even when only searching a room with six boxes scattered around, it can be difficult to keep track of which box has been searched, so imagine how tricky it can be to remember what you've searched in a large cargo shed with dozens of rows of shelving, or a multi-level engine room with storage areas and moving machinery. While you might not have access to such exciting areas with your dog, a village hall with stacked chairs, meeting rooms, cupboards and toilets can be just as complicated.

To help you search efficiently, and save you

Without a search plan it would be all too easy to miss contraband hidden in this cargo shed. (Courtesy Nick Saltmarsh via Flickr cc by 2.0)

having to remember what you *have* searched, a search plan made up of a series of patterns that you follow will prove very useful, and, in time, second nature. It will mean you won't have to worry about where you've been and where you need to go, and will allow you to concentrate fully on keeping your dog safe and watching for indications.

It also means that you are less likely to miss sections of the search area by simply following the plan.

These are the elements that make up the search plan, listed in the order they should be carried out –

- free search
- corners (or zigzag)
- perimeter
- interior

Stephanie Bell, one of the lovely handlers who attended our workshops, and came up with this clever mnemonic to help her remember the plan –

- **Find** (free)
- **Cleverly** (corners)
- **Placed** (perimeter)
- **Articles** (interior)

• **Free search (as previously described in Type of search)**

The free search should last as long as it needs to. That doesn't sound very helpful, I know, but you will develop a feel for how long it should continue. Once you have subtly moved your dog into all areas of the search, or when your dog looks at you as if to say 'what next?' you can then move on to the corners. Remember that, often, the free search is the first chance that your dog has to be in the search area, and become accustomed to it: have a look around and settle into searching. As a rough guide, less than a minute is all the time you should need for the free search, although this would change, of course, depending on size and complexity (how much is in there) of the search area. You will find that if you re-search the same area (a brand-new search using the same search area), your dog will be ready to move on to the corners earlier because he will be more familiar with the area second time around.

• **Corners**

The next step in the search plan is to cover corners, which is often where lots of articles, such as boxes, chairs, bags, etc, become piled

The free search.

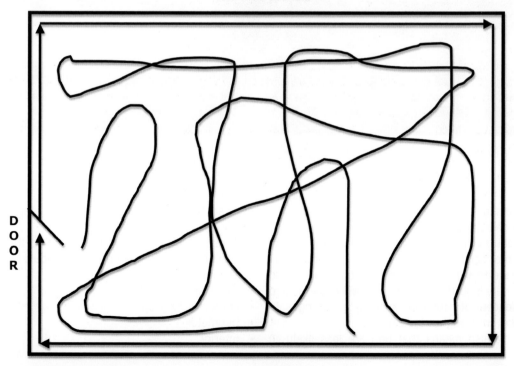

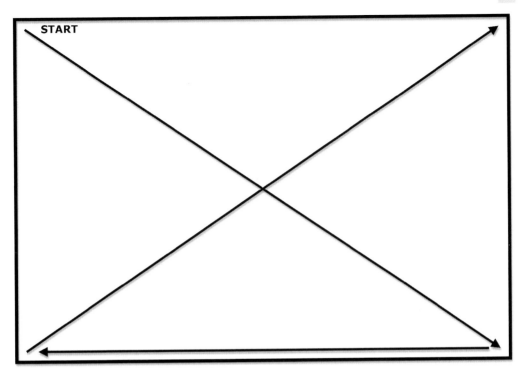

START

Corners pattern.

up, making it really easy to 'cut corners' and not properly search here. Searching corners is also the first occasion that you will ask your dog to carry out a directed search. This requires much greater concentration and thoroughness, which acts as a bridge between free and directed searching. Your dog goes from free to directed search in corner one; then free search again; then directed in corner two, and so on.

When you are ready to start the corners, go to the one nearest to you: efficient searches are better searches, so don't waste time walking across the area to the farthest corner.

As the free search ends, encourage your dog to 'Find it' by stepping to the right of the corner and gesturing toward it with your right hand, which should send him to search

in that corner. Help him to thoroughly search the corner by gesturing with your hand – high and low, indicating where his nose should go – making sure nothing is missed. If there are lots of articles the search area, once he has had a sniff of these, move what you need to give him easier access.

Just before he finishes searching the corner, quietly and quickly step out and back across the search area to the second corner, which is diagonally-opposite the first. By going to the diagonally-opposite corner your dog gets another chance to search through the middle of the search area which might result in an early find.

When he looks up from his first corner search, he will see you waiting at the second corner and head over. Say 'Find it,' gesturing

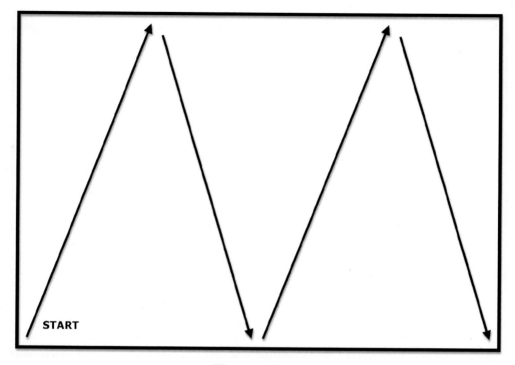

START

Zigzag pattern.

once again into the new corner with your right hand, and repeat the search you did in corner one, ie: working high and low, making sure he can easily access everything there is to search. Again, just before he completes corner two, move to the next corner along to your right.

Finally, move diagonally over to the last corner, which he can search when he's finished in corner three. Continue walking backwards as you move from corner to corner. If you turn your back to walk to the next corner you could miss an indication that your dog may give at the previous corner. By following this pattern, you will have searched all four corners and twice crossed through the middle of the search area.

When you begin to move to the next corner, don't call your dog, as he will get to the corner

before you, which puts you behind the action. You always want to be in front, guiding and supporting him, not following behind, and leaving it all to him. To help ensure you are always in the correct position with your dog in front of you as you present the area to him, remember to always move to your right. Begin in corner one, move right back across the diagonal, then move to your right to the next corner along, then right back across the middle again to the final corner. Right, right, right (unless, of course, you are working with your left hand, in which case it would be left, left, left).

Of course, some areas are too large to follow the diagonal pattern, because you couldn't physically move to each corner quickly or safely enough, plus you'd be too far away from him to spot any indications or provide assistance: if he wanted to jump up onto something, say. Other search areas might be long, and/or thin, and in situations like this you should substitute the diagonal pattern for a zigzag one.

As you are gesturing with the right hand and moving backwards, it can help you maintain position if you begin the zigzag at the bottom left corner of the area, so that you can always move to your right. As you come to the opposite boundary, turn right to face it so that you are all set to back over to the other side. As long as you always turn to your right as you zigzag along, you should be in the correct position.

So, starting at one corner, move diagonally across to the boundary of the area, then turn slightly right to move diagonally over to the opposite boundary. Keep doing this until you have zigzagged your way along the entire area from end to end. This approach does mean that you will miss two of the corners, but you will still cover the majority of space, and those missed corners can be included in the next step of the search plan.

When doing corners or zigzag, keep in mind what it is you want to search. You are searching the corners or spots along the boundary, not what is in the middle of the area. While you'd never want to discourage your dog from giving the middle area a sniff as he moves through it, don't specifically ask him to search anywhere except the corners and boundary spots during this stage of the search.

If the search area is an irregular shape or doesn't really have corners, just ensure that your perimeter search (coming up next) is very thorough.

• **Perimeter search**
After you have completed the corners, begin the perimeter search: a directed search, off-lead. Wherever possible, always choose the

same starting point each time, as having to remember a different one every time is more difficult than you might think. I always start at the point I entered to get into the search area, and work clockwise around the perimeter of the room, walking backwards and using my right hand, which will be closest to the wall or boundary, to suggest where my dog should put his nose. The direction is important as you want to guide your dog, watch him, and keep out of his way, so walk backwards, guide him with your right hand, and keep moving around the outer edge of the area.

By introducing the routine of always guiding with your right hand, you help your dog become an efficient searcher. Keep the search flowing; try not to stop and start too much – you should always be moving to the next spot as your dog is working. And don't worry: you will get used to walking backwards while still watching where you're going!

When working with an inexperienced dog, always show him specific objects to search, as pointing at thin air, floors or walls gives him very little to focus on in these early stages, and he won't know how to deal with them. Instead, suggest furniture, pictures, boxes, etc, for him to search by gesturing right onto those articles, not somewhere above them. Move quickly past 'dead' space which does not contain any articles that could provide a hiding place. As your dog becomes more experienced he will learn that things can be hidden under carpets, inside walls – and even on the ceiling!

• **Interior**
If your dog has not found anything, there are more articles still to find, or you want to be sure you've cleared the entire area during the free, corner and perimeter searches, it's time to search the *inside* of the area. This can be more difficult to search using a set routine as it depends on how the area is laid out.

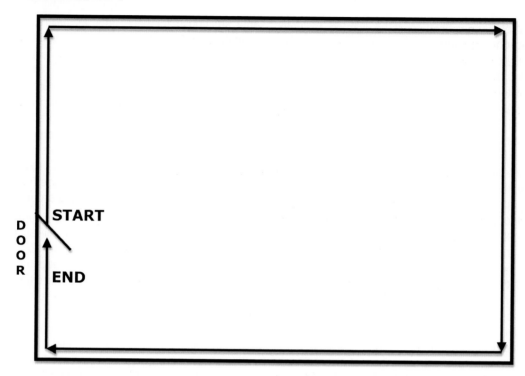

Perimeter pattern.

For example a classroom with chairs and desks in rows provides a logical pattern, whereas a room filled with chairs and desks set out randomly does not. The basic rule of thumb is to start at the same point where you began the perimeter search – at the entrance to the search area – and, working clockwise, search everything in your path around the area. In large areas you may end up working in a spiral from the edges into the middle, or up and down in lines. In smaller areas you may be able to access everything in a logical pattern in just one circuit. Whichever pattern you choose, be logical and stick to it, otherwise your dog may miss something.

If searching objects such as boxes, furniture or machinery in the interior of the area that are sufficiently large that it is necessary to walk around them to search them fully, do so in an anti-clockwise direction. The easiest way to remember which way to go is to always make sure that your right hand is closest to the article you are searching, be it a wall, car, box or sofa.

Here's the simple rule –

- If you are inside the object to be searched (usually a room), work clockwise
- If you are outside the object to be searched (such as furniture), work anti-clockwise

So, *inside* a room, work clockwise; *outside* a table, work anti-clockwise.

This may seem a little complicated at first, but once you get into the habit of working like this, you'll not even think about it, you'll just do it automatically. And if you always keep your right hand closest to the article/area you are searching you won't go wrong.

If you find that you are having to move your hand across your body, are behind your dog or he is behind you and you can't see him, then you're not in the right position. To correct your position, stand so that you and your dog are facing each other, get ready to gesture to your right with your right hand, and off you go again.

At the end of a search in which you have conducted a free search, covered the corners and perimeters, plus everything on the inside, you should have either found the article(s) or declared the area clear (blank). If the area is *not* blank but you've not found the article, check the troubleshooting section in chapter 7.

The thoroughness necessary for search patterns is more tiring for your dog, so begin with small areas, and gradually build up to searching for ten to fifteen minutes at a time.

Manage the search area

With many larger or more challenging areas, the most efficient way to search them is to divide them into smaller sections. Often, you can work the free search over the entire area, and then split the area into more manageable chunks, following the remaining three elements of a search pattern in each, before moving to the next. Splitting the entire search area into two, three or more manageable sections simplifies the search and reduces the risk of missing something.

I highly recommend practicing the search plan in various locations *without* your dog. This might seem a strange suggestion, but it is a

Interior pattern.

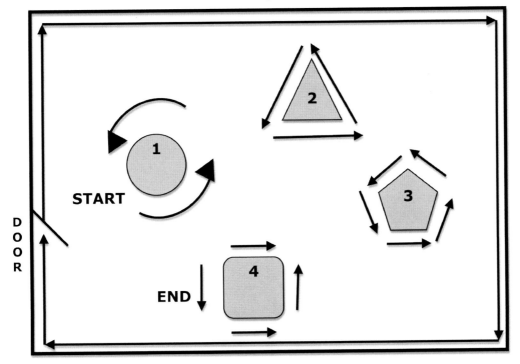

great way to learn and settle into the four-step routine. The next time you visit a friend, while she's in the kitchen making the coffee, why don't you walk the four patterns in her living room? Or when you're shopping, imagine how you'd split the store into manageable sections, and how you'd search each one (though I don't recommend zigzagging backwards down the aisle with your trolley!).

Consider how you would search areas that are irregularly shaped or which don't have distinct corners, and adapt your search pattern. For example, in a circular space you'd do a free search, then move straight to perimeter, and then interior: no corners or zigzag there. When doing a safety check in a new area is also a great time to plan your search and walk it through. This will help you anticipate your movement when you work your dog, leaving your mind clutter-free and better able to concentrate on spotting indications, and helping your dog find the scent.

Visit Hubble and Hattie on the web: www.hubbleandhattie.com
hubbleandhattie.blogspot.co.uk
• Details of all books • Special offers • Newsletter • New book news

Getting started

five

THIS MANUAL will teach you how to train an active indication for scentwork.

In theory, you can teach a dog an active indication on one scent and a passive on another. In practise, however, professional handlers would not do this, as they risk degrading both indications, confusing the dog, and potentially causing harm to them or their animal.

You also need to be a great trainer to achieve both indications, as this is extremely demanding on your dog and you, and I've yet to see it done properly: eg a dog finds one scent during the search and sits, but when he finds another during the same search he retrieves the article. If you manage this, I'd love to see the video. A dog would never be taught to find explosives and give a passive indication, and also search for drugs and give an active. What if he got the two mixed up?!

So make life easy for you and your dog: teach him an active indication.

The first step is to determine how your dog would like to be rewarded – with toys or food – as this dictates what he should search for.

Whichever reward is chosen, your dog will be hunting for the scent and not the article. This is an important point as some people get hung up on the erroneous thought that searching for food is easier, or somehow less 'valid' than searching for a non-food scent, when the principle is exactly the same. You are teaching your dog to locate specific scents, so not *all* herbs (which are a great scent choice as they are easily available in dried form, and are generally safe for your dog to sniff) if he is searching for catnip, just as not *all* foods if he is searching for cheese.

When you watch a dog scentworking, you have no idea what he is searching for – catnip or cheese – until he finds the article. If he's searching for catnip, he'll find a toy to play with; if he's searching for cheese, he'll find food that he can eat.

If your dog is a half-hearted toy tugger or a disinterested retriever, it's likely that food will be a better motivator. If a game at the end of the search is not your dog's thing, his motivation to search is reduced. If, however, he is an enthusiastic foodie, then the obvious

Dickens is more interested in the environment than the toy, so cheese would be a great search choice for him ...
(Courtesy Wayne Holt)

... whereas Poppy is clearly enjoying playing with a toy! (Courtesy Wayne Holt)

reward at the end of the search is finding the cheese.

Some dogs will very happily play with a toy at home or in places where they feel safe and comfortable, but bring them into a training hall, and suddenly they don't want to. For these dogs, safety is paramount, and playing can make some feel very vulnerable. In order to boost confidence and relaxation, food is a much better option. If this sounds like your dog and you are starting scentwork at home where he will usually play happily, begin by scenting some toys, but if starting in a hall or unfamiliar area, teach him to search for food. As his comfort and confidence grows, you can use food less often and toys more, if you wish. Whenever you see his confidence slip, use food. Avoid using scented toys and food in the same search, however, as this gives him the opportunity to ignore the one he likes

least in order to spend all his time searching for the one he likes best. So, only one scent per search.

You can also reward dogs who will look for scented toys with a food treat, if they are happy to retrieve and carry articles but don't want to play with them. But be firm: no retrieve, no treat. It's not enough for him to just look at the hide and then look at you for his treat; he needs to at least pick up the article before receiving his reward, otherwise his indication will be small and vague.

My belief is that it is both unfair and ridiculous to exclude dogs who don't enjoy games with toys from the joy of scentworking. The option to search for a specific food is what allows every breed and temperament to take part in scentwork. So, if your dog likes cheese more than chase, choose food. How to introduce food scent is explained later in this section.

Introducing the scent
Non-food searches

Once you are certain that your dog loves to play with toys, scent your chosen toy. For clarity and consistency I will assume that catnip is the chosen scent and a mouse the toy, as these are commonly used in my workshops and on my DVDs.

Begin by playing with your dog and the catnip-scented mouse, and make it a really exciting game, full of competition, energy and excitement. All the things you might have heard about never playing tug and not chasing your dog go out the window here: play the game your dog wants to play; give in to the fun. Skimming the mouse along the ground can encourage your dog to chase it, or tossing it in the air for your dog to catch is much more fun than waving it in front of his face.

Tug is a great game that many dogs enjoy, but take care to play safely. If you have a dog who chomps hard on the toy as he plays with it, use something long, or large enough that your hands are out of harm's way, such as a plaited fleece or a furry pencil case. Make sure when tugging that you physically come down to your dog's level: never tug upwards

Play with the scented mouse.
(Courtesy Bob Atkins/Your Dog Magazine)

Tease and tempt your dog with the toy to encourage play.
(Courtesy Bob Atkins/Your Dog Magazine)

Remember to use your left hand to play with the scented article so that your right hand remains scent-free. (Courtesy Bob Atkins/Your Dog Magazine)

Ensure you keep your dog's spine in alignment during tug games, to avoid possible injury to him. (Courtesy Bob Atkins/Your Dog Magazine)

as this puts all of your dog's body weight on his neck, which can be painful for him, and cause problems. Instead, play so that his body, neck and mouth are in a straight line with the toy and your hand. By keeping him aligned like this you can have an exciting but safe tug game.

Don't toss toys over his back or towards his body. Unless your dog is already an accomplished catcher, this often results in him having to jump and twist backward, which is very uncomfortable and potentially risky for him. Toss the toy so that it flies in front of him or slightly to one side so that he can move forward to catch it instead of twisting backwards.

Consider the flooring, too, as slippery floors and jumping dogs are not a good combination. Follow your dog's lead, as he will let you know how he likes to play. Some dogs love to just hold the mouse and wiggle over to you for cuddles and fuss. If this is your dog's favourite celebration, go with it. Be sensible, but have fun.

When the game reaches its peak and your dog is loving it, stop playing and take away the mouse. Place it in an unscented bag or container, and put it somewhere out of your dog's reach. This apparently mean action is necessary because you want your dog to associate the mouse with heaps of fun, and stopping the game at its most exciting point prevents him from becoming bored, and increases his desire to play with it again the next time he sees it.

Ask your dog to drop the mouse in the same way that you'd ask him to give up a ball or anything else he's carrying. If you have already taught a 'drop' or 'give' word, that's ideal, but if you normally swap the article for another toy or treats, feel free to do that. Never wrestle the toy from him or pry open

his mouth. Teach him to happily give up what he has as it makes life nicer for everyone.

After giving your dog a complete break from playing (all games; not just this one), a drink and a rest (you should both need it if the game was energetic enough), you are ready to begin 'throw-ins' – the important link between playing with the catnip mouse and searching for it – which is generally done in three steps. If you have somebody to help, they can entice your dog and toss the toy into the room for you at each step.

Throw-in: step 1

Using your living room as the search area, have a short game with your dog and the mouse in the hall. Then, holding your dog by his collar or, preferably, his harness, run him to the open living room door, and throw the mouse straight into the next room. Release him as you say 'Find it!' or whatever phrase you've chosen as the search cue, and follow him into the room as he rushes to catch and play with the mouse.

You need to be in there with him so you can engage him in an exciting game with the mouse, because, if you stay outside the room when he runs in, he'll suddenly find himself alone there, and that's no fun. Make this game intense but fairly short.

Okay, let's think about what you've just done.

First of all, you've reminded your dog that playing with the mouse is fun. Then, although maintaining the energy of the game by running to the living room door, you've introduced slight frustration by preventing him from running straight into the room as you have hold of his harness. This prompts him to jump into the search area with much more gusto than an energy-sapping 'sit-stay' instruction would. (If your dog has a wonderful, solid stay, don't use it now, but keep it for later when you have built motivation into the task, and

Throw the mouse into the next room ...
(Courtesy Bob Atkins/Your Dog Magazine)

60   **Detector Dog**

Use whichever room you plan to search as the venue for the throw-ins.
(Courtesy Bob Atkins/Your Dog Magazine)

... then send your dog after it.
(Courtesy Bob Atkins/Your Dog Magazine)

Bonzo grabs the mouse in the training hall during his first throw-in.
(Courtesy Wayne Holt)

are fine-tuning the final stages of working together.)

The mouse should be thrown into the room dead ahead of your dog so that he sees this, and also where it lands, and knows exactly where to go to retrieve it.

In order to maintain the energy, the instant you throw the mouse, give the search cue and release his harness. Your dog is set up for success; all you need do now is run into the room to play with him as soon as he picks up the mouse.

For Bonzo's second throw-in, the mouse is just around the corner instead of straight in front of him as he enters the room. (Courtesy Wayne Holt)

For step three, place the mouse behind something so that your dog has to use her nose rather than her eyes to find it.
(Courtesy Bob Atkins/Your Dog Magazine)

Cherry follows her nose to locate the scented mouse.
(Courtesy Bob Atkins/Your Dog Magazine)

Throw-in: step 2

Finish your game and take your dog back into the hall. Again holding his harness, throw the mouse back into the living room, but instead of throwing it straight into the room, throw it to the side so that when he runs in, he has to look to locate it rather than it being straight in front of him.

Give your 'Find it!' cue and release your dog. Follow him in as before and play with him and the mouse.

Throw-in: step 3

Finish your game and take your dog back into the hall. Leaving him there, take the mouse into the living room, closing the door behind you. Place the mouse behind something on the floor that is just to one side, such as a

Success! Cherry finds the mouse.
(Courtesy Bob Atkins/Your Dog Magazine)

footstool, magazine rack or cushion, as your dog enters the room. Simply place the mouse behind something at this point, rather than hide it, so that it's not too difficult for him to find.

In the previous two steps you have built trust, and he knows that when you say 'Find it!' there will always be a scented mouse for him to find. This time, when he sees you go into the room with the mouse, but doesn't see you throw it, he will trust that when you say 'Find it!' the mouse will be there somewhere.

You're now ready to let your dog into the room. As you open the door, say 'Find it!' and step back in the direction of the mouse. Should he look a little confused, say 'Find it!' again, moving towards and then past where the mouse is. Your movement should encourage your dog to move, too, when, hopefully, he will get a whiff of the scent, or even catch sight of the mouse. You can use your hand to gesture in the direction of the mouse, but don't point at it or directly show him where it is: instead, suggest an area for him to search, moving in the direction of the location, and sweeping your hand low over the hide. When he finds it, have the biggest game ever!

If your dog was confused by step 3, or didn't find the mouse, consider how you might tweak what you did in order for him to succeed, and then repeat step 3. For example, if your hand gesture was a little high, he may not have been sniffing low enough to scent the mouse. Hide the mouse again, and this time ensure your hand gesture is low enough that he can hit the scent. Or perhaps he was confused about where to look because you were standing too far back from the hide, in which case, repeat step 3 and this time move close to, and past, the hide to encourage your dog to follow, which gives him the best chance of finding the scent.

After successful completion of step 3, finish the game. Place the mouse in a bag or container, ready to be washed and re-scented before using it again, or to help maintain the scent it already has if you plan to do some more work later the same day. Remember not to put it back into your storage tin. Doing so will contaminate the other articles, the catnip, and the inside of the tin with your dog's slobbery scent and the scent from your hands.

The purpose of throw-ins is to gradually build the idea with your dog that the scented article is there to be found and played with: it's his introduction to searching for something. Don't worry that he is using his eyes rather than his nose in the first, second, and perhaps even third step of the throw-in: he's learning to search so must be set up to succeed. Building his trust that when you say 'Find it' there will always be something to find – and that he can rely on your support to locate it – are the important things here.

Food searches

Introducing your dog to searching using food as the scent article is achieved a little differently.

Firstly, choose the food (obviously, something that your dog likes). I strongly recommend you use cheese because it has some surprising properties, the main one being that it sticks to almost anything, which makes it fabulous for scentwork, and you are not as restricted about where you can hide it as you are with a toy. Cheese can be stuck to walls, fences, furniture, boxes, cars (for vehicle searches), plastic, wood ... the list goes on and on. In fact, during comprehensive research I've found that cheese will stick to almost everything apart from cold metal.

This capability is important because cheese that has been stuck inside the corner seam of a box will take your dog longer to eat, and so give you chance to see the indication and confirm the find (searching for a find that your dog has already located and eaten is frustrating for both of you!). And if he should scoff it before you get there, chances are there will be a smear of cheese left to show where it was hidden. Cheese can also be warmed in your hand and moulded like Plasticine® or modelling clay, which further increases the scent picture and makes it easier for your dog to find.

Use a mild cheddar or similar, though be aware that better quality cheddar may crumble as it contains less fat. Very fatty cheeses, such as Babybel or Edam, have too much fat, and don't have such a strong scent. Your dog won't be eating huge quantities of cheese when searching so it shouldn't affect his weight or well-being.

You can, of course, use other food, preferably something soft, smelly, and very sticky. Biscuits are not great for this stage of scentwork as they have a much smaller scent picture than cheese or other soft foods, but if your dog is on a very restricted diet, you can soak kibble in a little water, and, providing the search is fairly short, this will stick to some surfaces.

Once your dog is happily searching and can tolerate brief delays in eating his finds, hide the food inside safe containers which let out the scent but deny him access to the food until you facilitate this. You can use plastic tubs with holes in the lid, or pencil cases, or even plastic pipes with holes drilled in them. (Use 'soft' plastic rather than brittle plastic which can shatter and cause injury.) The idea is that

your dog brings the food-filled container out of the hide, and you then empty the food out of it for him eat. As with searching for non-food articles, ensure that you use a variety of containers so that your dog does not begin to *look* for the container rather than scent the food.

Do remember that, just as in searching for catnip, your dog will be searching for a specific odour, because he is not being trained to search for *all* food, but, in this instance, for mild cheddar. Eventually, once your dog is hooked on scentwork, you may even find that he ignores other foods he finds when searching for cheese. Consider the mess that Custom's dogs encounter when they search planes after long-haul flights, with food waste, and worse, on the seats, floors, seat pockets, etc. For untrained dogs this represents doggy delight, but working dogs simply ignore it. So don't chop and change the variety of cheese you use. Start with mild cheddar and stay with it.

The 'find it' game

Begin teaching your dog to sniff out cheese by playing the 'find it' game.

Cut some cheese into small pieces, and give your dog a piece. Don't ask him to do anything for it, just hand him some 'free' cheese. Then toss another piece onto the ground, close to where you are standing, and, as you do, say 'Find it,' or whatever your chosen scentwork phrase is. From now on, whenever you toss a piece of cheese to the ground, say 'find it' as you throw it. This will prompt your dog to look down and begin sniffing out the cheese: to sniff on cue.

What adds value to this game is that, once he has eaten the titbit of cheese, he will look at you, and, as the game progresses, will voluntarily return to you to see if you are going to throw him another piece. By waiting until he chooses to look at you, you are effectively

Food 'find it' game.
(Courtesy Bob Atkins/Your Dog Magazine)

Use the hand gesture to suggest the direction of search.
(Courtesy Wayne Holt)

rewarding the attention he is showing, and later, a recall. More on this to come, but, you can now begin to toss the cheese further away, gradually increasing the distance your dog has to travel to locate it.

Then you can introduce some direction by throwing it to your, left, right, or even behind you. Carry on with this for a minute or so and your dog will quickly learn that the 'find it' game is one he'll want to play again and again.

Once he is comfortable with the game at this level, start to throw the food around corners and behind things, to increase the search time and help him get used to finding the food in unexpected places, such as behind the coffee table or under a chair. As the cheese is now out of sight more often than not, help your dog find it by using your right hand to give direction and suggest areas for him to search.

It's important to always keep this guiding hand clean, but even more so when your dog is searching for cheese. If your hand smells of cheese, he has no reason to move past it in the direction you suggest, and, instead, will simply follow your hand. To be fair, dogs who have been trained using food rewards and lures are actually taught to do this, but now we are asking him for something slightly different: to work past our hand in the direction suggested by it.

Here, I've used chairs as a visual barrier, and the hand gesture to help the dog find the **cheese ...** (Courtesy Wayne Holt)

... which he quickly does! (Courtesy Wayne Holt)

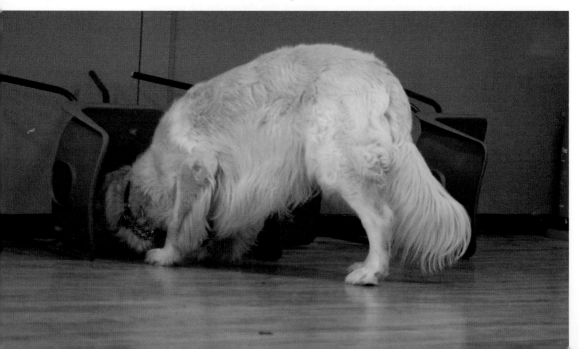

To encourage your dog to search low down, keep your hand low to the ground.
(Courtesy Bob Atkins/Your Dog Magazine)

Help your dog to put his nose down by sweeping your hand along the ground, palm up, tapping the ground with the backs of your fingers. As he puts his nose to the ground, sweep your hand out of the way and let him continue on in the direction of the tossed cheese. Make sure you don't have any bits of cheese still in your hand or this will distract him from the search, and encourage him to follow your hand.

Keeping your hand low to the ground encourages your dog to sniff at this level, whilst waving your hand in the air or pointing down will have him following your hand rather than moving away from it to find the cheese. Give him solid areas to search, such as behind a chair, under the table, or in a box instead of gesturing in the air, which he will find confusing.

It's well worth highlighting the usefulness of this game for all dogs. I use the 'find it' game to reward recalls, help dogs cope with traffic, build confidence around strangers, prevent them from eating horse/rabbit/deer poo, move past, not through, muddy puddles, and pay attention to me rather than other dogs. Even if your dog is scentworking for a non-food article, he can still play the 'find it' game with food. It is so adaptable and useful; a staple in my training toolbox.

If you do not intend to use scentwork as a team game (whereby you watch your dog search for the mouse or cheese rather than actively helping him find it), you need go no further, as you have taught the 'find it' cue, and your dog has learned that he will be rewarded with a game or the cheese. Job done!

But if you'd like to take this to the next step, read on ...

Once you have completed all the steps to introducing your dog to the scent, food or non-food, let him rest. Scentwork is very mentally tiring, and you don't want to push your dog too hard or try to make him learn too quickly.

Later, or even the following day, you can move to the next stage: first searches.

First searches

The first search you'll do will be a free search, which is when your dog is allowed to search the whole area with minimal guidance from you. Your job is to encourage him to continue searching, and to make sure he doesn't miss any part of the area.

Begin by hiding the scented mouse/cheese, ensuring that he can access the find when he locates it. You don't want him to find it but be unable to grab and play with it (or eat it, in the case of cheese), so hide the find at floor level: behind a chair, perhaps, or under a cushion on the floor. Cheese can be stuck to a chair or table leg close to the ground.

While you are hiding the article, leave your dog outside the room, behind a closed door.

When you are ready for him to search, go out to him so that when you open the door you can send him into the room with a 'Find it!' This search should be done in the same room that you used for the throw-ins or 'find it' game, as doing so allows the gradual layering of your dog's experiences, building on previous work, little by little. Changes can impede learning, so it's important that only one change occurs at a time, eg: sending him to search when he can see the article being thrown into a room to when he does not see it thrown.

Sweep your right hand into the room, gesturing towards potential hiding places, but not necessarily the actual hide at this stage. If your dog looks unsure, give him something definite to search: gesture close to, or even tap with the backs of your fingers, a specific article, such as a box or chair, rather than waving your hand in mid-air. Quickly move into the centre of the room, walking backwards so that you can watch him at all times during the search. You are looking for indications that he

has found the scent, as well as any sign that he needs some help.

While your dog is searching, encourage him ('good lad'), but don't distract or badger him by repeating the 'find it' cue too often. As long as he is sniffing and searching, there's no need to repeat it. Should he lift his head or look at you, this is the right time to remind him to 'find it' and give the hand gesture, which will motivate him to keep going, safe in the knowledge that he will find the article.

When you see an indication – a change in his behaviour or demeanour – ask the question 'Have you got something?' which will either prompt him to investigate further (yes, he thinks he's found something), or move away to search somewhere else (no, he doesn't think it is there).

We all know how curious dogs are: if we show interest in something they want to look at it, too. Therefore, as you ask the question, step away from your dog to allow him to answer the question honestly, without any influence from you, his handler. The simple act of stepping towards him as the question is asked can be enough to convince your dog that you know something he doesn't. He therefore looks more interested, causing you to think 'Yes! He's indicating,' and move even closer, reinforcing his belief that you *do* know something! This is all well and good if the article has been found, but, if not, is disappointing for your dog, and disillusioning for you.

So, if, having asked the question 'Have you got something?' and stepping away as you do so, your dog stays where he is, continuing to sniff and indicate, you can encourage him to get the find ('Go on; you get it; sort it out; where is it?'). He shouldn't need any physical assistance from you to reach the find as you should have placed it within easy reach for him. But if you have miscalculated, move in and make the toy more accessible by bringing it to the edge of the box if your dog is worried about sticking his head all the way inside; moving the cushion so that the mouse is only partially covered, or adjusting the furniture a little to give him better access to the hide.

When he eventually gets it, really let him know how pleased you are by praising him and playing an exciting game with the toy. After a short but enthusiastic game, take him from the room and hide the article again, or, if he has found the cheese, let him eat it, and, once it's all gone, praise him before taking him out of the room so that you can hide another piece of cheese.

Hide the article as before but in a different place in the same room. Send him into the room with 'find it,' and support him by moving around the room, repeating 'find it' in an encouraging voice only if he looks up or at you. Then, spot the indication, ask the question, move away, and get ready to play.

Obviously, if you are the one hiding the article, you know where it is, but, when searching, do not lead your dog to it, nor completely avoid it. Pretend you have no idea where it is hidden and let your dog search freely around the room. If you lead him to

it, he doesn't have the chance to search for himself, so won't have the fun of building his scentwork skills and confidence. It also means that you won't be observing him carefully enough, looking for those precious indications that become even more sought-after when you come to searches where you do not know where the article has been hidden. Likewise, if you avoid the area, he might completely miss the location, and the search will be too long and unrewarding.

If you have a willing assistant, ask them to hide the article, after giving them clear guidelines about where they should and should not place it. And ask them to stay with you while you search so that they can assist you and your dog should you need any help. For example, driving him into a blank area or inadvertently stepping forward as you ask the question can be prevented by your helper telling you the article is not there.

I recommend doing only three or four short searches at this point. Your dog is building experience as well as concentration. Put the scented article in a ziplock bag or container, ready to be washed and re-scented before it is used again.

Search
specifics

six

T O BEGIN with, searches should be for
very short periods only, and from the
brief search during the third step in
the throw-in sequence, to advanced searches
lasting for 30 or more minutes, there are
many stages. Search length will be dictated to
a degree by your dog's stamina, concentration
and confidence, all of which must be built on
gradually. Placing finds in impossible locations,
reducing the scent picture, and searching for
too long in the early stages of scentwork will
be detrimental to this objective.

Initial searches should be nice and
straightforward. Limit the number of things in
the area that could distract or confuse your
dog (the more there are, the more he has to
search). In my workshops I limit the number
of boxes I put out in the search area to a
maximum of six or so, so that a dog has only
to search these before he finds the article.

Searches do not always go to plan, of
course. You might believe that your setup
will enable a nice, quick find, but if your dog

Starter search area.

Starter search with Ella.

doesn't search in the order you think he will, he might have to investigate everything before he gets to the find. As his handler, your job is to gently guide him towards the hide, when appropriate.

For example, rather than letting him struggle, or risk him becoming frustrated, guide him towards the hide, and suggest he search there, simply by moving towards it and using a hand gesture. You may also repeat 'Find it' if you think he needs that extra encouragement to keep working. When he does locate and indicate on the find, ask the question 'Have you got something?,' stepping away as you do so ready for him to eat the food, or pull out the toy and have a game with you.

Each time that you suggest looking somewhere in particular, and your dog is successful as a result of your help, he learns that you can be a real asset to the search. Knowing this provides inexperienced dogs,

or those lacking in confidence generally, with great support, and can also encourage confident, independent dogs to pay attention to you. Independent dogs can start out by ignoring their handler, and searching on their own. While this may be fine for owners who do not wish to participate in the search (apart from hiding the article), for those who want to work with their dog and move on to more challenging searches, it's essential that he views you as a team-mate; a helper. As the challenge of the searches intensifies, you can work on this aspect of scentwork, encouraging your dog to pay attention to your suggestions.

Assistance like I've just described should not extend to telling your dog where the find is, or looking for it yourself in blind searches. Taking your dog to the find means that he has no need to search, as you are doing it for him! The consequence of this is that, in blind searches where neither of you knows where

the article is hidden (known as a double blind search), he may have trouble locating the find, and won't be able to rely on you to provide any help. So, suggest he looks somewhere, then watch for his indication.

The more often you can get somebody else to hide the article, the better, as it means you can concentrate on your dog, watching him and working with him. If you know where the find is, it can be difficult to accurately identify indications. You may *think* you see a change because your dog is close to the hide ... but is he really indicating?

It is for this reason that I prefer to use blind searches, where the handler does not know where the hide is, when first teaching scentwork. This is not always practical (if you are working alone, for example), so be alert to the danger of assuming you see things when you don't, and, equally, of avoiding areas for fear of leading the dog directly to the hide.

Work your dog as if you do not know where the hide is, and be guided only by his indications ... and not your assumptions.

At this stage in training, your dog should find something at every search, which should take between 30 seconds and a minute to ensure a quick find. Remember to reward your dog by playing a good game with the find, or help him get all the cheese out of the box. If you skimp on the reward, his incentive may wane. As he becomes more proficient, ask him to search a variety of containers, and not just cardboard (if that's what you've been using), and in a variety of areas. So, if you've been searching the living room, why not search the hallway or the dining room? In time, you can link areas together, and search the living room and the hall, and/or the dining room, increasing the search time as your dog's concentration and search stamina grows.

Next, introduce hides at different heights.

Small increases in height can modify the search.
(Courtesy Bob Atkins/Your Dog Magazine)

Searching the sofa. (Courtesy Bob Atkins/Your Dog Magazine)

Place the article on top of a radiator that is not on, or behind a curtain on the windowsill. Encourage your dog to use you to lean on so that if he needs to get up on his hind legs, he can rest his front legs on you while he searches at height. Some dogs are unwilling to do this (mostly if they have been taught not to jump up at people), so let them rest their front legs on a wall, radiator, etc, instead.

Give thought to where you do and do not want your dog to go. If you don't want him jumping up on furniture, for example, don't hide the article behind the sofa cushions, and if you don't want to encourage counter-surfing, don't hide it on kitchen worktops. Be sensible and practical, and also consider the safety aspects of the area he is searching. It's easy for your dog to become entangled in cables from lamps, the TV or computer, so don't place the find amongst them, or encourage your dog to search here. Think also about chemicals and cleaners, which are most often found in the kitchen, bathroom and outdoor

areas such as sheds and garages. Make sure they are safely out of reach, or choose not to search in certain areas.

For example, even though I know that dogs will generally ignore food whilst searching for other scents, I don't want to encourage my dog to work in the kitchen, so that room is out of bounds as a search area. Set your search areas according to safety and preference.

Intermediate searches

Stepping up the challenge of the search usually entails increasing search time, adding more elements to the search (such as height and variety of containers), and reducing the scent picture so that your dog has to work harder to locate the find. I advise that, if you've not already done so, now is the time to start working your dog in a harness, as you will need to be able to support him at height, or when searching anything unsteady. Also, when working directed searches on-lead, any restriction of the throat or head will affect the

Bertie searches a variety of containers.

A strong indication from Lexi.

efficiency of his search, so working him in a harness instead of a head collar or collar is highly recommended.

Begin by putting out two finds, which will allow him to continue searching the area after the first is located. When your dog brings out the first find, have a very brief game with him, dispose of the find (to your back pocket or out of the search area), and carry on with the search. Understandably, some dogs are a little perplexed when this first happens: they have found the article, after all, and have no idea there is another one out there! However, if you encourage him to search on and he subsequently finds a second article, his faith in you increases and you've grown in value as a team-mate. If he indicates the that your dog look in an area he hadn't previously considered searching, and bingo! he finds the article. This is by far the easiest way to encourage dogs to search new areas, heights and objects. Simply hide a scented article or piece of cheese and he will usually be happy to search there in future. A rich source of equipment to give height and variety to your scentwork is your local stationery shop, which will have all sorts of clips and hooks that you can use to loosely attach the article to the backs of curtains, chairs, clothes, etc. It may also have magnetic clips that you can use in vehicle searches, or anywhere with a metal surface that would make a suitable hide. And then there are pencil cases, inside which you can place the article (which provides another layer for the scent to permeate), or use *as* the article. The variety of materials – cloth, fake fur, plastic and rubber – that these come in makes for a diversity of challenges, both in location of the find and the retrieve aspect of the search.

Bags and clothing hanging on the backs of chairs or on hooks on the wall can make useful hides, too, although do not use coat stands or other freestanding articles as these are likely to be pulled over by dogs giving active indications. Do think carefully about placing finds in clothing, too, as they may become ripped or damaged when your dog retrieves the find. I like to use clothes that would otherwise be thrown away, rather than any I wear.

Height is very easy to achieve if you are using cheese because, as noted earlier, it sticks to most surfaces: under the windowsill, on the door, on the banister, under the car, beside the garage, on a fence. Cheese is super-flexible when used this way.

When introducing height, ensure that the article is within your dog's reach. If he begins air-scenting (sniffing the air) during the free search, verbally encourage him to follow his

Clip an article to the curtain for a high find. (Courtesy Bob Atkins/Your Dog Magazine)

location of a previous hide, tell him 'Good lad!' (acknowledging his correct indication), and then work him on. As your search area increases, you can put out several finds, working him on from each after a brief game.

Introduce height in a similar way. Suggest

The scented mouse has been hidden high in the tree ... but is still within Cherry's reach.
(Courtesy Bob Atkins/Your Dog Magazine)

nose. Ask 'Have you got something?' and, as he sticks with the air scent, gently praise and support him with 'Good lad, you get it, where is it? Clever dog!' If he doesn't hit the scent during the free search, when you are working the perimeter and inside of the area, suggest he looks higher when he is close to the hide. Suggesting height when he is far from the article can be counter-productive as he will not find anything, and so could quickly dismiss your suggestion to look higher up.

Once he has found something higher up, he will be keener to look here of his own accord. Over the next few searches, have one hide high and one lower during each search so that he is rewarded for checking high up, but doesn't forget to check low down, too. When introducing height, it's also worth considering very low hides. During initial searches, finds are often at a dog's nose level, and now is the time to begin placing them lower still: under mats or boxes; on skirting boards (cheese). This greater variety of hides keeps the searches fun whilst increasing the challenge

Ted finds some tasty cheese on the fence post.

for you both. Everywhere has the potential to be a hide: ceilings, behind furniture, in wall or flooring cavities, dado rails, windows, curtains, books – anywhere!

Another way to make the scent picture smaller, and so increase the challenge, is to hide the article inside multiple other articles, so that your dog has to sniff through layers of material rather than just one box or bag. Hide the toy or cheese inside a small box, and then place that inside a larger box. You can use baskets, basins and bags to layer the challenge: a box inside a bag inside a basin inside a basket will make for a tricky find, for example. As the handler, you should ensure that you give your dog access to the air inside all of these layers, so crack open boxes, lift basins just off the floor so that he can get his nose inside, and open bags, stepping back each time to allow him to search them thoroughly.

You can change a scent picture by varying the scented article. So, rather than just using material articles such as a toy mouse or strips of towel or fleece, try scenting pieces of wood, plastic, cork, or even metal. Scent them as before by placing them inside the tin containing the catnip. Ensure you select articles that are safe for your dog; if it's possible he may swallow articles or chew them, use bigger articles.

Your dog may not be as enthusiastic about playing with different articles as he is playing with the mouse, in which case, you have the choice of either praising him for retrieving the found article, then working on to complete the search, putting out an easy find at a later stage, or swapping the different article (a metal spoon, say) for a scented mouse so that he can have his usual game. Encourage your dog to pick up articles of different materials by playing with them before you scent them, just as you would any novel toy. Retrieving spoons or wood blocks in return for a treat or a game with a soft toy is a wonderful way to

The scented article can be placed inside a small box, which is then enclosed in the larger box.

help your dog happily bring unusual materials to you. Be inventive; be creative.

And, of course, just searching for longer increases the challenge: blank searches or large search areas can increase working time from 30 seconds to ten minutes.

When increasing the challenge for your dog, do so one aspect at a time. For example, you might decide to hide an article on a windowsill, at a higher level than you've used before, in which case, use an article that is at least mouse-sized, and which gives a good scent picture, rather than scenting a metal spoon or using a layered find. One new challenge at a time: there's no rush.

Vehicle searches (exterior)

These are great intermediate searches as they take place outdoors, so make a great introduction to this new area. Outdoor searches are more challenging due to the increased and sometimes more erratic airflow, which is why they are not great for initial searches.

For example, you could be searching a car where the article is hidden on the passenger-side rear wheel. The wind could easily bring the scent *under* the car so that the dog detects it on the other side, or at the front of the car. In such a case, it's up to the handler to spot the indication, and ask the question, allowing the dog, confident in his ability, to track back to the source of the scent, even though this means breaking away from the search pattern.

In essence, the vehicle search is simply an on-lead directed search. As with any search, use a set routine to help avoid confusion, ensure that everything has been searched properly, and make it possible to watch for indications. I recommend starting the search at the driver's door, just behind the wing mirror, because if you move on to doing interior vehicle searches, you can work your way around the car, opening the driver's door to let

Albert tells Elliot that he's found something on the wheel.

your dog inside when you arrive back there. Work around the car, moving anti-clockwise so that your guiding right hand is closest to the car, with your left holding the lead long and loose. Stand close to the vehicle, facing your dog, and move at his pace around it.

Before beginning a vehicle search set some limits. You don't want your dog to jump all over the paintwork, for example, so place your articles where this can't happen (wheels, hubcaps, wheelarches, bumpers or areas underneath the car).

There are lots of little lips under the bodies of most vehicles where you can sit or stick articles. Of vital importance is that you ensure your dog cannot sniff, inhale or come into contact with anything noxious or otherwise harmful, such as the petrol tank or a hot exhaust. A lead will help keep your dog safe should you be working in a car park or near a road on your driveway, as well as ensure he does not jump up onto the car when he is learning how to do vehicle searches.

Your first search should provide your dog with a quick, easy find. Place the article on top of the front, driver's-side tyre. When your dog gives you a puzzled look, as if to say, "Why are we standing beside our car; where are we going?" and "Did I hear you right, did you just say 'Find it'?" he will quickly understand the relevance of searching the car, and how toys, cheese, etc, can be found here, too

The first search should take you only from the bottom of the driver's door to the wheelarch to the tyre. For the next search, hide the article somewhere slightly further around the car so that your dog has to search about half of the vehicle. Finally, hide the article even further around the car so that he has to search nearly all of it.

The next stage is to secrete a couple of articles in the same search, so that your dog finds the first one, has a short game with it, then works on to find the second one, at which point he gets a bigger game.

As with all directed searches, when your dog indicates, step away and ask 'Have you got something?' Let him push past you if he's picked up the scent, making a mental note of the point in the search that he broke off so that, if he cannot track down the source of the scent (it may have been carried away when the wind direction changed, or it may be scattered due to blustery conditions), you

can go back to that breakpoint to resume the search. That way, nothing gets missed.

Once your dog realises that the vehicle is one big hide, he will be keen to get working. You may find on subsequent vehicle searches, that you do one circuit of the car almost as a free search, and then concentrate on the more detailed directed search on the second circuit.

Vehicle searches are fascinating because of the airflow around, under, and over the car. They really test a handler's skill in reading their dog, and the dog's skill in tracking the scent to the source.

Vehicle search (interior)

As a general rule, I do not recommend interior vehicle searches unless you have access to vehicles other than your own. The residual scent of the article within the car will remain for some time, which means that, if your dog travels in the car and is aware of the scentwork scent every time he does so, the scent will begin to lose its potency. It won't be as exciting to him because, although he can smell it, there's no search; no game; no reward for identifying it.

Then there is the safety aspect. You do not want to encourage your dog to jump around inside the car, whether or not it is stationary, as this would be chaotic and unsafe, and may ruin your dog's great 'settle' in the car. If he knows he's allowed to search the car and go wherever he wants, it will be difficult for him not to do it whenever he wants.

If you are able to have access to an alternative vehicle, search the exterior first, then let your dog into the car. Before starting the search, however, decide whether or not the boot space will be classed as exterior or interior.

Saloon car boots are usually best done during the exterior search, for example, and, if the parcel shelf is in place, hatchback and estate boots can be done during the exterior

search. Otherwise, they can be easily accessed from inside during the interior search. Don't allow your dog on, or lift him onto, the parcel shelf as it is likely to break, and will at the very best startle him if it gives way (and may cause injury). When deciding how to conduct the search, unlock all of the doors so that you can easily open them if you need to help your dog at any time.

If, during an exterior search your dog gives strong indications that the article is inside the car, let him into the vehicle (making a mental note of how much of the exterior has still to be searched). Unless you are searching trailers, caravans or limousines, there's unlikely to be enough space in the car for you and your dog, so direct him from outside the car, leaning in and suggesting places for him to look.

Try to be methodical: asking him to search first the front and then the back. Of course, this plan can quickly fall apart if he indicates early on in the search, but then has to track back to the source of the scent. Help him do this, using the drive-in technique as well as your voice to urge him on, and help him thoroughly investigate areas where he is indicating most strongly.

Interior car searches can be difficult due to the small area that your dog has to work in, and the high chance of the scent picture being fairly big – certainly during intermediate searches. Until the door is opened, the scent pools in the car, and the entire interior smells good to your dog. When everything smells of the scent it can be tricky for him to work through the scent picture to get to the source. Your dog will really appreciate your help to find this.

Baggage searches

Operational baggage searches take many forms –

- on the baggage belt that conveys bags

around the carousel from air side to the arrivals hall

- when searching bags in the pods that bring the bags from the aircraft

- bags can be lined up as they are unloaded from the pods but before they are placed on the baggage carousel

- specifically carried out on hand baggage, whereby selected travellers line up their bags in front of them

- without the bag's owner being aware of it, simply by the dog team walking through the arrivals lounge, departure lounge (especially if looking for money), along the railway platform or in the ferry terminal

Some of these scenarios are easier than others to recreate!

Begin by placing a selection of seven empty bags of various sizes, shapes, etc, in a line on the floor (use handbags, suitcases, sports bags, satchels, bags made of leather, canvas, hessian, plastic). Consider how difficult it is for the air to circulate out of and through the different materials of each bag as you plan where to hide the article. Hard shell cases and briefcases, such as Samsonite or Delsey, are much more difficult for the dog to work, so leave them out of his searches for now. Hessian and material bags are easier, so are a great choice for the first baggage search.

Leave enough space between the bags for your dog to walk around them: ensure they are not touching. Remember that each new search type throws up its own challenges, so should be set up to allow your dog to be successful. Bags which are touching each other at this stage in the search make it more difficult for your dog to identify which bag

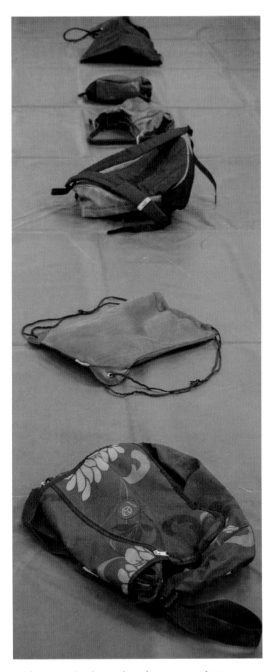

Line up the bags leaving space between each one. (Use this same set-up for starter postal searches.)

Work backwards along the bags.

contains the article, as both bags could easily become contaminated.

Ideally, begin baggage searches with your dog on a lead to help him focus on searching *just* the bags, and not the entire room. As with the car search, initially, quickly walk around the line of bags, as in a free search. If, however, your dog settles quickly into searching, go straight into a directed search.

Work backwards, moving anti-clockwise around the line of bags so that your guiding hand is closest to the bags; let your dog have a good sniff at each. If he wants to walk over the bags, that's fine, as this helps push air through the bag, and so increases scent picture size. As your dog works the line of bags, should he indicate, ask the usual question 'Have you got something?' and back away. If he has got something and stays with the bag, help him to precisely locate the find by opening the bag and/or turning it over to allow him to access the article. Once you've opened the bag, step back to give your dog space to search it thoroughly.

Dogs are great at telling us exactly where in the bag the article is hidden. Observe him carefully so that you can see which pocket or opening he hones in on. Then, if he needs help (perhaps the article is in a zipped compartment), step in, open the zip, and step back again.

Crowding your dog while trying to assist him is counterproductive. Give him access and guidance, but don't search the bag for him, or hover over him as he works to locate the find. If he appears worried about putting his head in the bag, or has trouble locating the find in the first place, change to hiding the article under rather than inside the bag.

If your dog doesn't indicate on any of the bags, help him search more thoroughly by turning over the bags over; perhaps even opening them a little so that he can have an extra good sniff, but don't be tempted to look

into the bags yourself as you open them up. Your dog will find the article and just needs a little time and opportunity.

This may be the first time that you see your dog searching very thoroughly, and, if he has to sniff through several layers of material in a rucksack, he will take longer to search the bag than you are probably used to. Having become accustomed to how long he usually needs to sniff an article, you may be tempted to ask the question too soon in this search. Ask yourself whether he is just being thorough and taking his time, or whether he is indicating. Delay asking the question for a few seconds until you are sure of the answer.

Once you have used a bag, you can, perhaps, use it again for one more search, but then it needs to be washed. It can go into the washing machine at 60°C/140°F to eradicate the smell of you and your dog. There's likely to be some residual smell of the scent you want your dog to find, but it will be very faint. Do not hide a different scent in that bag, though, and only ever use it with the original scent. Combining the smells of more than one scent will diminish your dog's ability to accurately identify a particular scent.

Mix up the order of the bags between each search so that your dog doesn't have a preconceived idea of their positions.

Source bags for searches from friends and family, local car boot sales and jumble sales, and auction houses and lost property offices.

Outdoor searches

As discussed in the vehicle search section, working outdoors increases the environmental challenge, and decreases the control you have over temperature, wind direction, and other distractions.

Start by defining the area you intend to search. Look for landmarks to form boundaries, be they fences, a tree, a plant pot or a path.

Be prepared for your dog to range more

widely than with indoor searches. Allow him this wide range but don't follow him out of the designated search area. By allowing him to range a little you give him the opportunity to maximise his use of wind direction (he will naturally use that to his advantage), and hopefully get a whiff of the desired scent. By staying within the search area yourself, you can draw him back into this in order to follow back to source the scent he's caught on the wind, and minimise wasted energy spent searching outside the area.

As with the first car search, your dog will not be expecting to find his scent article in this new area. Areas where your dog has a reward history, or strong expectation of carrying out a particular activity, add an extra element to initial searches. He needs to trust that when you give the search cue, 'Find it!' no matter where he is, he will be guaranteed to find the article. But that trust doesn't come

cheap, so, when he gives you the benefit of the doubt and begins to search outdoors, it's essential he has a quick, easy find initially, as this will reward his trust in you, and reinforce the connection between following the search cue and finding the article.

Before placing the article, check the area for holes, glass, debris, etc, so that neither of you is injured. You shouldn't be working backward outdoors as it's all too easy to trip or fall over. Covering larger areas means that working backward is not practical, in any case, and, instead, you'll be mostly walking forward and sideways, with some backward movement, so that you can observe your dog, *and* watch where you're going. Check what is and is not moveable, such as unstable logs, industrial machinery, or vehicles (such as those found on farms or haulage yards), and fixtures and fittings in dilapidated areas. Never assume anything; always check for hazards before the search commences, rocking and moving objects to check for stability rather than just looking at them.

Outdoor searches provide plenty of scope for hides: in trees and bushes, under pots, logs or undergrowth, behind rocks and boulders, in ditches, in the sand, and along the hedge. Safety is your primary concern, of course, followed by access for your dog. Do not hide the article somewhere that you cannot access – you absolutely do not want your dog to become stuck somewhere that you cannot access to help him, so don't throw the article into a tiny space behind buildings, or far into the undergrowth. Also, don't hide it in brambles, nettles, or other plants that could injure your dog.

Consider the weather conditions. Hot, dry weather will give larger scent pictures than will damp, cold conditions. Wind is the main

Breckin finds some cheese in the bales.

factor to consider. If you begin your search upwind of the hide, the scent may be carried *toward* your dog, and so provide him with the chance of an early indication. Downwind hides, where the scent will be carried away from your dog, may require more detailed searching. Alternatively your dog could run on ahead until he is upwind of the hide, and then work backward.

This is why you need to be on your toes, thinking all the time about the scent picture and understanding why your dog is searching in particular ways: eg ranging wide, moving away from the hide, or working more slowly than usual.

An interesting aspect to working outdoors is that a dog will find scent, or vapour, trails much more noticeably. These trails are left by you/your assistant as you walk along holding the scented article, and are specifically targeted by some firearms and explosives (FX) detector dogs in areas such as airports, where criminals have explosives on their body or in their baggage. As they move through the airport, the dog picks up the trail and tracks it right to the criminal. I have seen dogs go straight to the article in some pretty challenging environments simply because they followed the vapour trail.

To minimise this, and make the search more of a challenge, carry the article inside the sealed tin or container, only taking it out when you come to the spot where you intend to hide it. Alternatively, walk around the area, stopping at several spots before actually placing the article so that, even if your dog picks up the trail, he is not taken immediately to the hide.

Of course, if your dog needs some help during outdoor searches, you can use the trail to provide this, simply by carrying the scented article in your hand, rather than in the sealed container.

Postal searches

Postal searches carried out by companion dogs have been extremely enlightening for me, and have made me appreciate just how good my – and all – Customs dogs are.

Simply put, postal searches involve a dog searching postal sacks full of mail, but, in order to consider some of the factors involved, it's necessary to break that down –

• The postal sack. These are mostly made of woven propylene, and appear to hold the scent of everywhere they've been and everything they've touched. (I assume this is due to the weave rather than the propylene.) Woven fabrics capture and retain scent in all the tiny gaps within the weave, and if used sacks are employed, the combination of all the scents on them can prove enough of a challenge, never mind once they also contain post *and* a scented article

• The contents. Not every piece of post is the same when it comes to scent. I tend to split the contents into three categories –

A paper envelopes – the easiest to search when the bag is not very full, and allow the scent to move through the envelope quickly. Cheap envelopes (brown ones that contain bills) are easier for the scent to move through and soak into than high quality or embossed paper). However, when densely packed into a postal bag, sandwiched with others and with little movement, envelopes can hold and retain scent very effectively

B small packets, boxes, padded envelopes – small, cheap, cardboard boxes will easily absorb scent, and also release it easily, just as with cheap envelopes. Lots of boxes within a bag can make for a nice, intermediate challenge; adding padded envelopes (plastic bubble wrap encased in shiny paper that holds the scent inside) increases the difficulty

C shiny, printed leaflets, flyers, junk mail – this is the trickiest as it takes time for the shiny material to absorb the scent. Once it does, however, it retains it, so scent can easily be trapped between leaflets and flyers, making it very difficult for your dog to find, especially when the bag is densely packed with junk mail

The simplest way to begin a postal search is to lay out a row of empty sacks – say five or six – and hide the article under, not in, one of the sacks. Using the on-lead directed search technique, with your dog, work your way along the bags, around the top and back down them, giving him lots of time to have a good sniff. Have a really good game with him at the end when he finds the article.

Once you've completed a few successful postal searches in this way, place the article inside the otherwise empty sack, tipping it on end to allow the article to fall out when your dog gives a solid indication on the correct bag. Most dogs will look at the top of the bag as you tip it up, so ask him again to 'Find it' by gesturing towards the floor so that he finds the article as it drops out.

A postal search is a lot like a baggage search in style and technique: moving around the bags (to help 'puff' out the scent), or turning them over to allow your dog to search more thoroughly.

After the initial session with empty bags, begin adding some envelopes to all of the bags so they are all the same. Then place the article in the sack *with* the envelopes at first, only progressing to placing it *inside*

an envelope *inside* the bag once your dog is confidently searching the bags, and indicating on the correct one. Gradually increase the number of envelopes and boxes you add to the bags. You can also increase the number of bags.

Remember, once a bag has contained a scented article, it is contaminated, so this bag – and its contents – can only be used again if the article is actually hidden in it, and even then it should only be used a couple more times so that any other contamination (usually from the dog) does not become associated with the article.

Postal bags wash very well at 60°C/140°F in the machine, which should reduce contamination level to a minimum, and allow you to use them again.

When your dog indicates on the correct sack, tip out the contents and allow him to search through them to locate the article. This means that you carry out two searches: one to identify the correct bag and a second to identify the correct envelope.

If your dog cannot locate the correct envelope, help him perform a systematic search of the sack's content by placing the envelopes in a line, along which he can search. Another way is to spread them out so that your dog doesn't have to search through piles of post. Always let him have a good sniff before moving the contents, and try not to move them while he is sniffing, otherwise you may inadvertently move the find away from him, or, at the very least, cause air disturbance which will make his search more difficult.

The search becomes more challenging as you increase the number of bags and the number of envelopes and boxes in the bags. You do not want to decrease the amount of scent at this juncture, so continue to use mouse-sized articles, and don't hide them inside multiple layers of post. This can be

done later when your dog is confidently – and successfully – searching the postal sacks.

Source postal sacks from your local post office; sometimes your postman can help you out. or you can buy unused sacks, not necessarily postal – rubble sacks, for example – from many gardening shops, as well as online.

How to make the search thorough
One of the most common handler errors I see as teams increase the challenge is lack of attention to detail. Not being thorough can make the difference between your dog finding the article and missing it, but how to do that without going over and over the same area?

As ever, the answer is simple: watch your dog; really look at where he is sniffing; check if he runs past the area or if he actually works it. Does he physically move into the space but his mind is engaged elsewhere? To help your dog pay attention to all of the details, practice directed searches where the hides are dotted in and around those areas most likely to be missed during searches. These are often the corners, various heights (if you and your dog have been searching at high levels, lower search areas can be skimmed or missed, and vice versa).

Not moving/lifting/opening articles that retain scent, rather than allowing free airflow, is part of making the search thorough, as your dog will not yet be experienced enough to detect such small scent pictures. Overall, the most common mistake is for the handler to assume that the hide cannot be in a particular place, and so actively or subconsciously avoid it. Scent can be anywhere, but it's not the handler's job to find it: only to give their dog access to everything in order to ensure the area has been searched once, thoroughly.

Setting a time limit on searching an area can be a good way to ensure you are thorough and efficient. Repeatedly going over areas or articles can deter a dog: asking your dog to search an area again, when he has already done so and knows it is clear, can be demoralizing for both of you. Remember to split the search area into manageable sections. Several smaller searches within the designated area allow you to complete each section then forget about it, freeing your mind to fully concentrate on the next section.

Advanced searches
At this stage you are providing your dog with very challenging searches, which, for some, may be a step too far. Dogs who can successfully work at this advanced level need to be confident, have a strong drive to work, and trust their handler to support them. If you find that your dog's motivation to search begins to wane as the searches become more difficult, go back to the level that he enjoyed, and work on providing variety at that level and below.

It's also important to remember that, just because the two of you can work at an advanced level, it's not necessary for all searches and finds to be at that level. Mix it up so that sometimes the finds are quick and easy, and at other times your dog has to search for a long time before finding anything.

Set the search level wherever it needs to be to –

• address an issue you want to work on or improve

• provide the most fun and reward for your dog

Advanced searches minimize the scent picture by using very small scented articles, such as scraps of material, small pieces of plastic piping, and lagging, and, ultimately, simply smearing the scent onto surfaces, or using scented labels to stick inside bags, boxes and basins, and onto floors, furniture and fences.

Obviously, smaller quantities of scent give off less smell, make smaller scent pictures, and thus are harder to locate. Alternatively, hide larger articles deeper within hides: inside boxes inside bags, wrapped up, inside plastic and wood, deep inside full postal bags, or suitcases containing clothes, for example.

The better you understand scent and how it moves, the greater insight you will have into the level of difficulty you are presenting your dog with.

The handler's role is heightened at this level, too. Thorough searches are essential, so don't skip areas, cut corners, or assume it's a blank search. Scent that has been smeared onto a surface, or labels/slips of paper that

Elliot watches as Albert scans around to pinpoint the scent source ...

**... and has it! He's looking right at the metal spanner that is the scented item.
Clever boy!**

have been inserted into cracks will often not be visible, so search everything and everywhere.

When searching for pure scent rather than actual articles, secondary finds are helpful. When your dog hits the scent, acknowledge this and praise him, then work on to find an article further on in the search. Or you can quickly throw a scented article at the spot where he has indicated on the scent. Of course, at this stage your dog should be able to work one or two searches with no external reward (the search itself becomes the reward), except for praise from you. Very challenging. And very realistic.

Before you or your helper get too carried away with being devious with your hides, you do need to be aware of certain facts before you start the search –

- whether or not your dog can access the finds without help

- if you are searching for a tiny article (a plaster, say) or just a smudge, so that you don't drive-in your dog for something that isn't there. (In these situations it's good to have a scented article in your back pocket ready to put out when needed.)

Indoor advanced searches

Hide scented labels, such as small or cut up Post-it® notes, fabric plasters, pipe cleaners, or tiny articles such as half a scented cotton bud that your dog will not be able to actually retrieve in cracks around cupboard or entrance doors, windows, and behind pictures or signs. And you can hide a variety of articles in unusual places such as in drawers and cupboards, and under rugs – anywhere, really, that there's space.

The very best hides are those in articles that are normally in an area. In an office this could include files, hole punches, pen pots and

This is a very challenging box search area: lots of boxes filling the space gives great scope for tricky hides.

bookcases. Imagine scenting a piece of material and hiding it in the hole punch reservoir (after emptying out all of the punched paper first!), or amongst a pile of papers in a box file, or even in an old telephone. In a garage, tools and tool boxes, bits of machinery or old car parts that do not jeopardise your dog's safety (no have sharp edges or lubricants/fluids, etc). Scent a spanner, for example, or hide a toy mouse inside an old pipe. Everywhere can be a hiding place. Be creative, be inventive, but, firstly, *be safe*.

You can make a search area either very barren or very busy; both will provide a challenge for your dog. Litter the area with whatever you think will distract him – toys, other dogs or children, depending on your resources. Or the ultimate distraction for many dogs – food! Operational dogs have to search kitchens, galleys, post-flight passenger planes and domestic houses, so introducing food in containers or on tables, etc, can make for a super challenging search area, depending on how tempting your dog would find this. As always, work safely. If your dog is likely to guard food or run off with it, use a different distraction.

Baggage
Cases or bags

You can work on all types of skills with these, recreating hand baggage or luggage. Fill hand baggage with books, make-up bags, pencil cases, etc, but don't put gadgets or phones inside as these might get broken if your dog is working on active indications. On the other hand, if you have old equipment that won't harm your dog, and you don't mind if it becomes damaged, go for it.

Think like a smuggler. Clothing that is thrown into a case will provide a good level of difficulty, and rolling it will step it up again. Folding it neatly and filling the case to the

Hide the catnip inside the pocket of an old pair of jeans ...

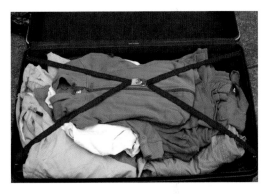

... pack the jeans into the case ...

... then have your dog search all the baggage to see if he can detect which one contains the catnip.

brim will be the most realistic scenario – and also the most difficult. The more layers the scent needs to work through, the trickier the search. And to add a further layer of difficulty, don't open the case's fastenings, but let your dog to search with zips, latches and locks secured.

If you have access to hard shell suitcases, you'll learn just how well you've trained your dog. Ask him to walk over to the case, and compress the top to force air out of the zip closure or rubber seal in the middle. Scent will travel out with the expelled air.

During the initial part of the search, line up the bags close enough to touch each other, and, as the search continues, move them around to give your dog better access to them. Open the zip a little as your dog arrives at each case, letting him get the first whiff of scent as the air inside the case finds the opening.

If you do a search with sealed baggage, ie you don't open it, simply praise your dog for indicating on the correct bag, remove it from the search, and work on. Once the search is complete, sit a toy mouse in one of the bags,

leaving the zip or catch open so that when he searches here, your dog can access the article. If you want to open the bags then just have an article hidden inside one. Put something inside the pocket of an old jacket, or folded up in some socks or gloves. Or secrete it in an inside compartment of a rucksack. Once your dog identifies the correct bag, he then gets a second search of the contents inside in order to locate the article.

Postal

Adding more post to the sacks, and carefully deciding on what type of post will instantly increase the challenge of postal searches. Try lifting a full postal sack: you'll no doubt find it surprisingly heavy. The weight of the post compresses the scent, and the density of the contents makes it difficult for air – and therefore the scent – to circulate around the bag's contents. The more plastic (as in padded bags), or glossy paper (as in junk mail) that you add to the sack, the more difficult the search becomes.

Instead of having the bags lined up, arrange them in a big pile that your dog has to rifle

Natasha and Toby tackle an advanced postal search.

Linda and Kaiden search a grassed area ...

through. You will still be on hand to move the bags and assist in the search, but this simple change in presentation of articles will add a twist to the search. (This presentation is better done off-lead.)

Outdoor advanced searches

You can really vary hide heights when working outdoors, and use fences, hedges, walls, equipment, machinery, bushes, trees: whatever the location offers.

Don't overlook 'blank' areas. The classic one is grass. If you are working in grassed or slate/stone-covered areas, the hide could be in the middle of it, under grass or stones. Often when working outdoors, handlers concentrate on working the perimeters, but the middle area can be just as challenging. You can even

... Bev and Luco search among the stones ...

... and Luco pulls the find from beneath them.

bury the articles – not deeply but certainly below the surface. Start at about 5cm (2 inches), and gradually increase to first 10cm (4 inches), and then maybe 15cm (6 inches), depending on how well your dog manages to find the articles. Ensure you disturb several locations so that your dog isn't drawn to the hide because of disturbance there, rather than the scent. For example, if you're hiding the article under pebbles, scuff up the pebbles all over that area. These searches can be really fun!

Scent discrimination as a specific exercise

During each and every search your dog is constantly discriminating between scents, looking for the one he associates with his reward. Everything has its own scent, plus contamination from whatever it has come into contact with, be that your scent, the cat, the children, the smell of last night's dinner, the plug-in air freshener, etc, etc.

At this stage in his scentwork career it's useful – and fun – to test your dog to ensure that you have taught him to search for the scent, and not the scented article. Hide unscented articles (a piece of material or toy mouse), and articles with non-trained scents in addition to the actual scent that your dog is trained to find. If he indicates on the wrong article, move him on and continue searching.

If he consistently gives false indications, go back a few steps and remind him of the scent you want him to find by scenting a greater variety of articles so that he doesn't associate a particular article with the scent.

Pare this down a little by using identical hides. Set up a row of five identical boxes/jars/containers. Place an unscented article in one hide and a scented article in another. Then ask your dog to work the line.

He may well linger a little longer at the unscented article than at empty containers. Watch carefully to check he's not just interested and being thorough rather than actually indicating when he stays at the same container for longer. Increase the number of scented and unscented articles as your dog continues to search successfully. If he's unsuccessful, keep things simple, and pare it back a bit by putting out just three containers: one empty; one containing a non-scented article, and one containing the scented article.

Next, try putting out a scented article and an article with a distinct, non-trained scent to see if he can discriminate between the two. Bear in mind that everything has a scent, so your dog will be discriminating between scents all the time during every single search. By adding a particularly strong scent that you *do not* want your dog to indicate on, you increase the challenge. Stronger scent = bigger scent picture = more chance that your dog will find it interesting.

This is a good challenge for you, as handler, too. You can see that your dog is smelling the new scent, but can you tell whether he is indicating? Smelling and indicating are not the same things, of course. You might smell a cake baking in the oven, but you don't necessarily act on this by walking to the oven ...

Note
Remember, some companion dogs who do not have the high search drive of professional

Tamsin and Lelki work hard to find the target scent amongst identical containers in the grass.

working dogs can come unstuck when the scent picture is reduced, or when secondary aids are introduced. It's important to determine your dog's level and not ask him to work beyond this.

Appendix 1
Troubleshooting

My dog picks up random, non-scented articles

If your dog begins to pick up random objects during a search, this can be because he is frustrated or over-excited: he will need calm support from you in order to resume searching confidently and properly, rather than guessing which object you want him to retrieve.

If you can, continue searching, ignoring the object that your dog has picked up. As he begins to use his nose, he may drop this: after all, if you don't value it, it's of no use to him. Alternatively, you can take the object from him and then carry on searching, discretely giving it to an assistant or disposing of it outside the search area. On no account should you scold your dog for picking it up, as he is trying to find the scented article, and if you scold him for making a mistake, he may lose confidence and the desire to continue searching.

Frustration can kick in if the search has gone on too long for your dog's level of experience. If this is the case, either place an additional article in the area for him to discover quickly, or conduct a more thorough search of the area around the article.

If you try the latter approach and your dog does not indicate, even though he is on top of the article, quickly put out another article for him. The problem may be that he isn't sure what he is looking for; the article has several competing scents on it; or the airflow around the find is causing confusion. Whatever the reason, note it down so that, as his confidence grows, you can revisit the situation in order to work through it.

Following up incidents like this with a couple of simple, quick fire, known searches will allow you to restore your dog's confidence quickly and efficiently. Don't lead him to the find, but make more pointed suggestions about which areas are worthy of closer inspection or multiple scans.

The above situation is a great example of when a good assistant can be invaluable. If they have placed the article for you, they can direct you to specific areas if your dog is becoming frustrated or demoralized.

They need not tell you the article's actual location, but can suggest that you search, say, just the left of the area, or only in the middle of it. They can also have a second article ready to hide for you should the need arise, or take the incorrect article from you and remove it from the search area.

I have also seen this behaviour when a dog hits the scent very quickly but the handler misses his indication. This can send the dog into a highly agitated and confused state: he doesn't know what he should be looking for because he has been called away or ignored when he located the correct scent. This issue can be addressed by carrying out several, quick fire, known searches, as described above, with an easy-to-retrieve article, that is just sitting in an open box or behind a table. Of course, the problem here is not with the dog but the handler, who must improve their observational skills and be very clear about what they are looking for. Videoing searches can be a great help with this.

My dog is confused and won't search the cardboard boxes

This generally happens when dogs have been taught an alternative behaviour (ie non-scentwork) involving boxes. I can always tell whether a dog has been taught to step inside the box, or put his paw on it, or stand on it.

I recall one Irish Setter who worked his way around the boxes in the search area, standing on each one, looking very pleased with himself when he did so. His owner confirmed that he'd been taught to do this, and that he really enjoyed it. The answer? Remove all the boxes from the room. Instead, this dog searched chairs during the workshop, and worked beautifully, finding every bit of cheese we hid for him. So, if previous training adds confusion, remove the object and replace it with something more appropriate.

Some dogs are worried by boxes, and don't want to touch them or put their heads inside. If yours displays this cautious behaviour it can mean that he is a little anxious, or doesn't cope well in new situations. Talking Dogs Scentwork® can help build your dog's confidence by teaching him that it's very worthwhile for him to put his head into a box if it results in him finding the article. Build confidence by using completely open boxes at first; play fun games by repeatedly tossing the article into open boxes for him to fetch, or cheese for him to eat, and do this in full view of your dog. This process is about building confidence around unusual objects; not about scentworking. Building confidence in this way can permeate to other areas of his life.

If you are asking too much of your dog and he remains worried about the boxes, or any other objects, then the answer is simple – remove them from the area.

My dog works too quickly

Speed when searching is only detrimental if your dog is going too fast to find the article. Adjust your pace to match that of your dog. Working too slowly is likely to result in your dog ignoring you, and leaving you behind. You don't need to sprint around the area, but plan ahead and anticipate where your dog is likely to go, moving quickly to the areas you want him to cover; not waiting for him to get there and then following him – one of the most common handling errors I see.

Some dogs work very well at speed, appearing not to be working, even, but the test is whether when they go over the hide, they catch the scent and work it thoroughly. If your dog does this, then his pace is fine, but if he is not actually scenting efficiently, it will take longer to locate the article, causing frustration for your dog, and you to question his search skills.

I have found that the best way to address this is to present the dog with more challenging search areas. Place more boxes and containers in the area; increase the size of the area, and the variety of hide locations to include those both high and low. Use the layering technique of placing the article inside a couple of boxes to reduce the scent picture. Or use chairs and other objects to form a puzzle for dogs who rip up the boxes in their excitement to locate the article. A dog should quickly realise that he has to be more thorough in order to find the prize, and most will naturally slow their pace. By controlling the hide and the search area, you, the handler, give your dog a reason to slow down without impeding his progress or dampening his enthusiasm.

Some dogs do need extra help to slow down and search more thoroughly, and on-lead directed searches can really help them to focus on more specific areas, rather than trying to tackle the entire area in one go. Never use the lead to physically slow your dog, but only to minimise the choice of search areas.

My dog ignores me

Some dogs have learned to work without their handler's assistance, whilst others *think* they can do it on their own. In both cases, the dog should appreciate the relevance of the handler, who will help him find the article more quickly by suggesting areas that he might not have searched. The handler might even suggest areas that have already been searched, and – hey presto! – there's the article! A handler's active participation in a search that results in the dog finding the article in an area suggested by the handler will quickly alert him to the advantages of keeping an eye on his handler, and what he is doing.

If you find that, despite helping your dog find the article more quickly, he still ignores you, think about how you are working. Maybe you're moving too slowly and are a beat behind the rhythm of the search, in which case, pick up the pace, and try to lead the search more by using the search plan. The search patterns in the plan assist with keeping the search flowing. Too much starting and stopping whilst you decide where to go next may result in your dog moving on ... and leaving you behind.

I am unsure of the indication (indication or interest?)

When a dog hits a scent, changes in his demeanour and body language are indications. When a dog is merely showing interest, he is investigating whether or not he has found the scent. The more layers he has to sniff through, the longer he will take to work the article.

Handlers get used to the rhythm of their dog working, and learn to recognize when he's staying at an article or area longer than usual. In simple searches, this can often be because he's indicating on the scent, while, in more challenging searches, it can often be because he's working through more distractions and obstacles to locate the scent.

Dogs indicate in a variety of ways, as mentioned earlier in the book, but one indication is universal: intensity. A great way to distinguish interest from indication is to look at how intense your dog is, especially across his shoulders. When he hits the scent his body will become more rigid: harder; less fluid than when he's just showing interest. His focus becomes much sharper, and often his whole body will orient in the direction of the scent: his ears, head, eyes and shoulders will turn to point in the direction of the hide. If he's only interested, you don't see this intense focus, as he will be trying to pin down what he's detected.

The very best way to learn to spot the difference between interest and indication is to film your searches so that you can play them back at your leisure. In this way, you can really see what's happening, which can often be difficult to do mid-search. Watching the footage allows the picture to become very clear. You can even set up experiments to help you learn the difference. Using two or more boxes or containers, fill each with scrunched-up newspaper. In one only (ensure you know which one), hide the scented article/cheese.

The air and scent have to navigate around and through the newspaper, making for more interesting hides, meaning that your dog should have to search them for longer in order to figure out which one holds the scented article. This allows you more time to observe what it is your dog actually does as he searches each box, enabling you to better distinguish interest from indication. (If your dog is already a proficient scentworker, close the boxes to minimize the openings that air flows out of to just one or two holes (that you can make), or seams (the top seam where the lid flaps meet, for example).

My dog appears lacklustre in his search, or simply ignores the article

Some dogs seem not to enjoy the search, whilst others enjoy the search so much that, when they find the article, they almost ignore it to carry on searching, as the search is more rewarding than the actual find. This behaviour can be the result of a dog not loving the result of finding the article.

The easiest fix is to increase the excitement, duration and fun of the game, or change the reward that comes after the dog hears his reward 'mark' (a clicker or a word that tells him 'Yes, well done; you got it right!'). Often, though, it is the scented article or chosen food that, rather than being a great reward for searching, is actually a disincentive. Consider how you'd feel at the end of the month if you received a certificate commending you for all your hard work instead of a pay cheque. Wouldn't you feel short-changed - cheated, even? Your dog can experience this same sense of disappointment if, at the end of the search, he finds a catnip-scented mouse when playing with toys isn't really what he likes to do. You would prefer to receive cash; he might prefer to receive cheese.

There's little point working on with a dog who's half-hearted about searching because he finds a toy at the end, when changing the find to a food that he likes means he will be genuinely enthusiastic and happy to search. A view exists that teaching a dog to find food is not as valid, impressive or skilled as finding a non-food scent, but, to put it bluntly, this is nonsense. Both categories of find have their own distinctive scent, and a dog finds them by successfully identifying that scent. The only difference is that when he finds the non-food scent he will play with or retrieve the article, and when he finds the food article he will eat it. To deny a dog an article he actually wants to find in favour of one his handler would prefer is to take the fun out of scentwork.

You can build more drive for the non-food article, especially if your dog already likes to play but could do with being a bit more enthusiastic about the game, by clicking and treating for any attention he shows to the article, building up to a solid search and retrieve. The true strength of this learned behaviour will become apparent as the searches become more challenging: it has to be super-strong to drive your dog to search for the article over long periods, or dig it out from tough hides. Personally, I would rather allow my dog to search for something he naturally values.

My dog doesn't pick up the article

Go back to basics and work on the retrieve

exercise to resolve this one. This is how I teach the retrieve –

1 Choose a toy that your dog finds easy to pick up and carry.

2 Begin by having a really exuberant, exciting game with the toy. Get your dog's enthusiasm really going by enticing him with the toy, offering it but taking it back before he gets to it, and wiggling it along the ground. Pushing a toy directly at your dog or towards his mouth will not encourage him to play, usually, but moving the toy like a small prey animal should do.

3 Next, throw the toy a short distance, encouraging your dog to chase after and pick up the toy. Run alongside him as if in competition to get the toy. If your dog doesn't pick up the toy, quickly grab it and throw it again. If your dog thinks that you want the toy he will be more motivated to try and get it first. Once your dog has the toy, do not try to touch the toy, or take it away from him: you want him to have it and enjoy playing with it. The 'drop' will come later.

4 Run backwards in an excited and encouraging way so that your dog follows you while carrying the toy. If he doesn't want to come to you, encourage him to do so by clapping your hands, dropping down to one knee, and opening your arms to make a welcoming target. If he comes, reward this with a big fuss or a titbit, but still not touching the toy.

5 Once your dog is reliably bringing the toy to you, introduce the word 'fetch' as you toss the toy so that he associates the word with the action of running to pick up the toy.

6 The next step is to ask him to drop the toy, either into your hand or onto the ground. If he's still unsure about this, revise the drop routine (see below).

7 If you have been working on steps 1-6 on-lead, you are now ready to repeat these steps off-lead. This means that you can run towards the toy without the danger of holding him back with the lead if he runs faster than you!

8 Next, off-lead, throw the toy a short distance and encourage your dog to 'fetch' and pick up the toy. Begin to run alongside him as if in competition to get the toy, but rather than running all the way to the toy, hang back as your dog passes you so that he reaches it while you are still a little way off. Then, when he picks up the toy, run backwards, encouraging him to come to you with the toy. Gradually reduce the distance you run towards the toy until the point where you stay still while your dog chases the toy.

My dog will not bring me the toy, or won't let go of it if he does

Go back to basics and work on the 'drop' exercise to resolve this one. This is how I teach the 'drop' –

1 When playing with a toy, offer your dog a titbit by holding it at the end of his nose, so that he swaps the toy for the titbit. If you are playing a tuggy game, keep hold of the toy, but stop pulling when you present the titbit. Tip: make no attempt to touch the toy when he drops it but leave it close by him as he eats the titbit so that he can immediately resume the game. If, when your dog drops the toy, you immediately whip it away, he will be less likely to drop it next time. Leaving the toy beside him

means that he gets the titbit *and* the toy, a win-win proposition that he'd be mad to turn down!

2 Once your dog is reliably dropping the toy the instant he sees the titbit, you can add the verbal cue 'drop.' Say 'drop' then produce the titbit as before and swap it for the toy.

3 Now try saying 'drop' and only produce the titbit once your dog has dropped the toy.

4 As the 'drop' becomes more reliable, phase out the titbit altogether: your dog's reward for dropping the toy will be getting it back again.

Practise the 'drop' cue with a variety of toys. If your dog needs some help in relinquishing the toy, try working with a less exciting toy or a tastier treat: he's more likely to want to hang on to his favourite toy than his least favourite. Also, at the start, always return the toy to him to prevent him thinking that dropping the toy automatically means he will lose it. This is important because, in an emergency situation, you may need him to immediately let go of whatever he has when asked, usually with the expectation of a reward. If you've not practised 'drop,' he may worry that you will scold him, take away his 'treasure,' or both, in which case he might guard the article.

Never trick your dog into relinquishing an article; never grab for it, and always give treats freely, sometimes dropping them on the floor, letting your dog drop his toy, eat the treats, and then pick up the toy again. The next time that you drop the treats your dog will be likely to happily drop his toy, safe in the knowledge that you are not going to take it away from him. Drop more treats in a line that leads away from the toy to the point that you can calmly pick it up without your dog being concerned.

Once you have a reliable 'drop' for the food reward, use this at the end of your searches. When your dog finds the article and brings it to you, reward him with a food treat.

Appendix 2
References
Resources
Glossary

eight

References

How Scent and Airflow Works
http://houndandthefound.wordpress.com/2012/02/22/how-scent-and-airflow-works/

Kinetic Theory of Gases
http://chemwiki.ucdavis.edu/Physical_Chemistry/Physical_Properties_of_Matter/Gases/Kinetic_Theory_of_Gases

Structure and function of the vomeronasal organ, The Journal of Experimental Biology 201
Kjell B, Doving and Didier Trotier, 2913-2925 (1998)

Division of Labor
White, Steve, 2011

Canine Ergonomics: The Science of Working Dogs
2009, Helton, William, S (Ed), CRC Press, ISBN: 978-1420079913

The Canine Sense of Smell (The Whole Dog Journal)
Kidd, Randy, DVM, PhD: http://www.whole-dog-journal.com/issues/7_11/features/Canine-Sense-of-Smell_15668-1.html

What does space smell like?
http://www.educatinghumanity.com/2012/08/Space-Smells-NASA-is-Reproducing-the-Odor.html

What does space smell like?
http://www.inquisitr.com/287901/what-does-space-smell-like-nasa-astronauts-explain-the-stench/

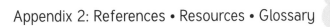

Resources

The home of Talking Dogs Scentwork®
www.scentwork.com

Catac working dog harness
www.catac.co.uk

Karenswood, working dog equipment
www.karenswood.co.uk

Kong®
www.kongcompany.com

Sue Sternberg, shelter dog and body language expert
www.suesternberg.com

Glossary

Active (aka 'proactive') – the dog makes contact with/retrieves the find

Article (aka 'find') – the scented object you want your dog to find

Blank search – when there is no pre-placed find/article

Blind search – when the handler does not know the location of the hide

Clear – to clear an area is to search it thoroughly before declaring that no scented articles remain within it

Directed search – a thorough, systematic, detailed search

Double blind search – where neither the handler nor the dog knows the location of the hide (if a handler knows where the hide is, he or she can sometimes subconsciously influence the dog)

Drive-in – verbal commentary to help maintain the dog's drive to precisely locate the find

Find (see 'article')

Free search – when the dog searches with minimal obvious guidance from the handler

Hide – place where the article is hidden

Known search – when the handler knows the location of the hide

Passive – the dog indicates by coming to a stop (can be a sit, down or stare) at the hide, but does not come into contact with the find

Proactive (see 'active')

Scent/vapour trail – when scent lingers in the air, allowing the dog to follow it to source

Scent picture – the plume or movement of scent that the dog detects

Secondary article/find – a find put out as a reward, usually mid-search, for completing a blank search/when a reward is required

Throw-in – the process of introducing the dog to a new scent

Think you know how it's done?

When Kac Young adopted a rescue dog called
Talulah, she consulted behaviourist Lisa Tenzin-
Dolma on all things dog-related. Lisa's observations
and guidance make an entertaining and informative
book that will appeal to both new and seasoned dog
guardians.

Hardback • 17x22cm • 120 pages • 80 colour images
• ISBN 978-1-787110-59-5 • £12.99*

Introducing Ollie and Nina, the delightful doggy duo ... and their daft Dad who writes about them!

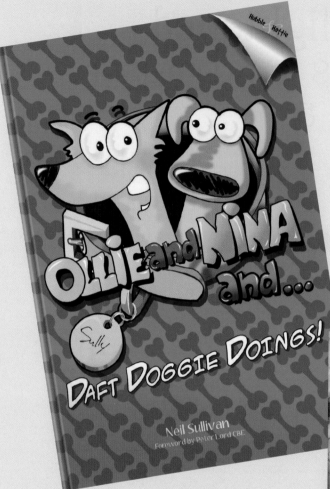

Ollie and Nina are *real* dogs and do what all *real* dogs do, but their daft Dad has taken the liberty of recording their silly goings-on in a cartoon strip.
Their stories are real, of course, though told with just a pinch of artistic licence, you understand ...

Hardback • 17x25cm • 64 pages • 50 colour images • ISBN 978-1-787110-65-6 • £9.99*

Worzel Wooface needs little introduction, luffly boykin that he is. Now, this enormous Lurcher with issues has penned his third literary offering, which is just as funny, just as true-to-life, and just as heartbreaking as his previous two offerings!

Paperback • 15.2x22.5cm • 144 pages • 50 colour • 3 mono images • ISBN 978-1-787110-58-8 • £9.99*

TWO FABULOUS, TRUE-LIFE BOOKS ABOUT THE WAYS THAT DOGS, AND OTHER (RATHER UNLIKELY) ANIMALS, HELP US ...

UNLEASHING the healing power of ANIMALS

True stories about therapy animals – and what they do for us

Dale Preece-Kelly

Hubble & Hattie

Chronicling the journeys of nine animals and one human, this book demonstrates how human-animal connection can lead to a relationship that is both therapeutic and healing, regardless of species.

Paperback • 15.2x22.5cm • 80 pages • 20 colour • 12 mono images • ISBN 978-1-845849-56-6 • £9.99*

HOUNDS WHO HEAL ...

people & dogs

It's a kind of MAGIC!

Chris Kent
Foreword by Dr Daniel Allen

Hubble & Hattie

The desire for human connection is a fundamental need. For some, however, the closest they come to this is with a dog. This is the story of six abandoned dogs, who ended up living together, and inspiring the development of the unique K9 Project.

Paperback • 15.2x22.5cm • 112 pages • 50 colour & 35 mono images • ISBN 978-1-845849-73-3 • £9.99*

Index

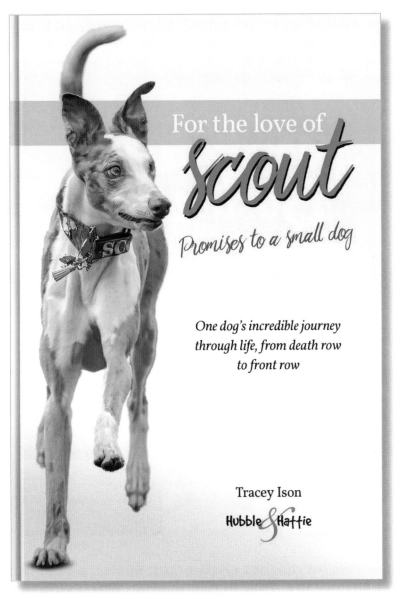

Boisterous Beagles and bothersome boats – adventures on the waterways of England, Ireland, and Europe!

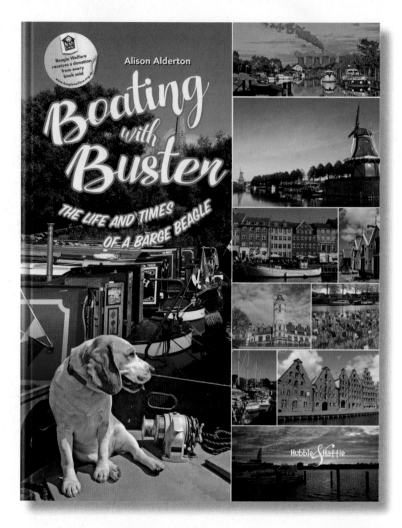

When her world reaches crisis point, Buster, a beagle puppy, enters Alison's life. This, in conjunction with living on Lily, a Dutch barge, soon brings about a welcome change in fortunes. Buster's larger than life escapades are colourfully portrayed in this moving book of canine companionship on the waterways of England, Ireland, and Europe.

Paperback • 17x22cm • 224 pages
• 100 colour images • ISBN 978-1-845849-72-6 • £14.99*